That Patchwork Place®

Appliqué in Bloom

Gabrielle Swain

Credits

Editor-in-Chief . . . . Barbara Weiland
Technical Editor . . . . Laura M. Reinstatler
Managing Editor . . . . Greg Sharp
Copy Editors . . . . Liz McGehee
Miriam Bulmer
Proofreaders . . . . Tina Cook
Leslie Phillips
Design Director . . . . Judy Petry
Text and Cover Designer . . . . Cheryl Senecal
Photographer . . . . Brent Kane
Illustrators . . . . Laurel Strand
Stephanie Benson

Library of Congress Cataloging-in-Publication Data

Swain, Gabrielle
    Appliqué in bloom / Gabrielle Swain.
        p. cm.
    ISBN 1-56477-076-1 :
    1. Appliqué—Patterns. 2. Flowers in art. 3. Patchwork quilts.
I. Title.
TT779.S97 1994
746.46—dc20   94-31132
                                                            CIP

Acknowledgments

While working on this project, I had the support of many people. I can never repay them for all that they have done, nor can I go on without mentioning them here. My gratitude to:

Barbara Hartman and Eugenia Barnes, for keeping my feet to the fire and convincing me that this project should be done.

Sandy Barker, for giving me the opportunity to test teach these patterns.

All the "girls" at the quilt shop, for listening and looking throughout the project.

My husband, Ronnie, for believing in my obsession and living with threads on everything.

Charles, for encouraging words and being a voice of reason to his siblings.

Craig, for teaching me how to use the computer and for keeping the house from falling down around us.

Chris, for always making me laugh at the darkest times and for constantly telling me, "Mom, you can draw."

Thomas, for doing without a mom during all this and still giving me hugs in spite of the danger of being stuck by needles and pins.

Jeannette and Harlan Swain, my "in-laws," for accepting and loving their weird daughter-in-law all these years.

Sue Hausmann and Viking Husqvarna for their support and for making a great machine.

Most of all, a special thanks to everyone at That Patchwork Place, for giving me the thrill of a lifetime— the opportunity to share all this with other quiltmakers.

I couldn't have done it without all of you. You will always hold a special place in my heart.

Table of Contents

INTRODUCTION

At the Start

Everything about quiltmaking excites me. From brain to frame, no matter which technique is used, each quilt bears the signature of its maker. Whether we design our own quilts or re-create from patterns, the colors, fabrics, and techniques we choose say something about us.

We find ourselves drawn to a particular palette and use those colors over and over in a multitude of ways—each time expressing something new about ourselves. Some of us piece our quilts, finding endless pleasure in the process. Others appliqué to achieve the look we desire.

My particular passion is appliqué, for a variety of reasons. Appliqué is portable, requiring very little equipment, so it can go everywhere with me. Its painterly nature provides unlimited imagery. More important, it is very forgiving. If there is a "mistake," you can simply apply another shape over the problem and continue.

The patterns included in this book grew out of my love for appliqué. They are a study in both style and technique. Flowers and floral arrangements have long been a source of inspiration for needleworkers in all media. The joyous array of color and shapes in each flower offers unlimited possibilities for designing quilts.

While designing these blocks, I developed certain criteria to create a particular look. These criteria were: that the arrangement be asymmetrical, that there be a "ground" of leaves or flowers to provide a backdrop for the primary or "focus" flowers, and that there be a variety of flowers within each block.

Until recently, nature had never been a major source of inspiration for my work, but since working with floral appliqué, it is all I can think of doing. Whether you use the designs in this book exactly or use them as a jumping-off place for an adaptation of your own, I hope nature continues to excite you as a possibility for design.

The Whole Truth

Contemporary floral appliqué began for me one spring day in the Amon G. Carter Museum of Western Art in Fort Worth, Texas. Barbara Hartman, a fellow quiltmaker, and I were taken by surprise as we walked into one of the exhibition spaces. On the wall was a still-life floral painting. The arrangement of the flowers was impeccable and the variety among them was delightful. The background included a sky full of stormy clouds and a river with whitecaps starting to peak. It was breathtaking.

"Your next quilt should be a still life of some kind—maybe flowers." An innocent statement on Barbara's part, but the exact moment when I should have run for cover.

Barbara can get me into more trouble than anyone else I know. She has my best interests at heart and I go along with her suggestions willingly—never stopping to question the ramifications. I trust her implicitly. "Floral appliqué—that has possibilities; use a new design approach." The conversation continued throughout lunch and during the drive home. I was already rushing toward what has proven to be one of the most demanding, yet rewarding experiences a quiltmaker could have.

In July 1992, the design process began. In August of that same year, the actual sewing started; and in September, nineteen students began a six-month class to test the patterns.

Like most instructors, I believe that I have been fortunate to have some of the most talented and patient students ever to walk into a classroom. The photographs included in the Gallery are testimony to their talent and skill. Helen Ruth Brandhurst, Peggy Cord, Ruth Cottrell, Susan Elliott, Linda Gillespie, Marilyn Mowry, and Dee Shaffer have been invaluable in completing samples for this book.

"Your next quilt should be a still life of some kind— maybe flowers." An innocent statement on Barbara's part, but the exact moment when I should have run for cover.

The following pages include the results of Barbara's few innocent words. (Innocent, hah! She knew exactly what she was doing—feeding the flame of my obsession with appliqué!) I hope that these patterns throw some logs on your fire as well.

COLOR AND FABRICS

We all have favorite colors and develop a personal palette from these favorites. Some quiltmakers work in primary or bright colors; others love pastels. A common palette in many of my quilts is black, red, and white. I love the drama and high contrast created by these colors. I know a quiltmaker who uses lime green as a neutral, and does it quite successfully.

With each new quilt, we start by choosing colors and fabrics to complement the design. Whether lime green or orange, each palette is uniquely individual, limited only by the needs of each specific project. Color is a fascinating subject that deserves intensive study by all quiltmakers. For our purposes, color discussion will relate to the blocks in this book.

Floral appliqué offers unlimited choices for using a wide variety of both colors and fabrics. Nature is a perfect guide when developing a palette. A trip to a favorite nursery or florist or a walk outside can give the best perspective on color in nature. Nature blends yellow with green, purple with fuchsia, and often in the same plant. The more color incorporated into the floral blocks, the more exciting they will be.

Green is the foundation color for any floral appliqué fabric collection. Passing up a green of any color or value is difficult for me, and buying less than a half-yard piece is sure to cause regret later. Some "must-buys" are yellow green, blue green, true green, gray green, and olive drab. Using a wide range of greens brings a more realistic feeling to floral appliqué. Look at the color variations within grass: you will find one green upon another, depending on the season.

You will need different values of green to create turned leaves and to show the difference between new leaf growth and older, fuller leaves. Value, the lightness or darkness of a color, is essential in all quiltmaking, and floral appliqué is no exception. A leaf's underside is often much lighter or darker than its top. As leaves age, the sun or water will often bleach out spots of color within the leaf. Use this natural phenomenon to your advantage; combine the darkest values with medium and light. Also, try changing a green's value and color from stem to leaves on the same flower for a more natural effect.

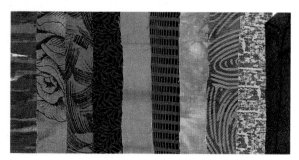

Greens ranging from yellow green, blue green, true green, gray green, and olive drab

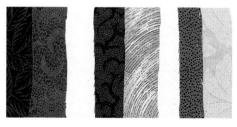

Values ranging from dark green over medium green; dark green over light green; medium green over light green

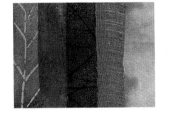

Flowers gain added dimension by changing in value from petal to petal. Think of how the light changes the shading on flowers or how flowers change colors as they grow from buds to blossoms. Many flowers have deeper hues in the inner petals and lighter values in the outer petals. Roses are a good example of this particular pattern. The inner petals of a pink rose may be a brighter, darker color than outer petals that have been exposed to the sunlight for a while. Any appliquéd blossom can be made darker at the center to create the illusion of depth.

Fall pallette: gold, rust, brown, yellow, orange

Values of gold from dark to light

When working on background leaves or flowers, using a variety of colors will create a more exciting field for the focus flowers. In Pattern 3, Maple Leaves, Gourds, and Anemones on page 48, the maple leaves in the background could be done in values of one color, but a mixture of colors would give the block an extra punch. Fall provides a vast range of colors—don't be shy about including the entire spectrum.

This theory can also be applied to any grouping of the same flowers. Anemones and primroses appear as background flowers in some of the blocks. Both of these particular flowers grow in red, yellow, orange, blue, pink, and purple. What could be more exciting than to appliqué a mix of these colors into this portion of the design?

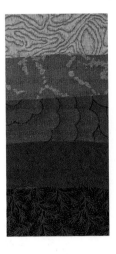

Values of red, blue, yellow, purple, and orange

Values of blue, light to dark

Values of red, light to dark

Often I stumble across something that simplifies my life. One of these "stumbles" happened while I was working on these floral blocks; I discovered seed catalogs. These catalogs are a good reference for identifying color in each variety of flower. Books on gardening or flower arranging from the library are also valuable resources.

For the most part, the flowers in the floral blocks in this book appear as they do in nature, but there is no reason they can't become fantasy flowers. Ruth Cottrell's quilt "Rosehurst—Christine's English Garden," shown on page 40, was a continuing surprise as she progressed through the blocks. Each new fabric she used opened endless possibilities for the entire class. As the artist, you are creating your own garden. Try making peonies in the wildest of batik fabrics. Select colors ranging from golds and oranges to the traditional reds and purples for berries and grapes. Refer to the color photographs of each block in this book to help provide ideas for your own work.

Complementaries: red and green, blue and orange, yellow and purple

When working on color for the patterns, the simplest approach can often be the most effective. Work with complementary colors: red and green, blue and orange, yellow and purple.

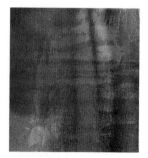

Triads: red, yellow, and blue; purple, orange, and green; magenta, turquoise, and gold

Try triad combinations of purple, green, and orange; red, yellow, and blue; or turquoise, magenta, and yellow.

Remember, the more color in the block, the more exciting the work—you won't regret it.

A few words about fabric selection must accompany any discussion of color in quiltmaking. Use 100% cotton (no blends) for appliqué: cotton is easy to work with, folds under nicely for needle-turn appliqué, and is available in a wide variety of prints and colors. However, don't be afraid to try silks and other fibers if they have the qualities that you are seeking. While other fibers and weaves may require more care when sewing, they can add a delightful preciousness to your work.

Some of the most useful fabrics for floral appliqué are fabrics with thicker threads or different weave structures, such as cotton sateen, damask, or silk. These fabrics add texture and sparkle to any piece, but they can be difficult to handle. I revised some techniques so that I wouldn't have to exclude any fabrics from my work. Normally, for needle-turn appliqué, the smaller the seam allowance, the better, but when working with "softer" fabrics, the seam allowance must be increased to a full ¼" wide. This prevents pesky stray threads that want to go "boing" and stand straight up, from being difficult. The extra seam allowance also provides stability to these weaves.

For the flowers and leaves, try everything from hand-dyed and marbled fabrics to huge scale or small geometric prints. Start looking for the flowers hidden in the fabrics. You will be amazed at the range of fabrics that can be included in floral work.

New to the market in recent years are hand-dyed batik fabrics. The color changes in each fabric are beautiful and provide many cuts from one purchase. Tie-dyed and airbrushed fabrics also can be used to create special effects. With these specialty fabrics, you can shade a single petal from one color or value to another easily.

Airbrushed fabric

Batik fabric

Large-scale prints also provide a variety of cuts from a single fabric. Leaves and petals cut from the same fabric ensure color blending. Look at these large-scale prints in 2"-square segments to help visualize all the cuts available in that particular fabric. Selective cutting is a useful technique to develop for floral appliqué, stretching a single piece of fabric into many uses.

These large-scale prints also make beautiful vines. Try to see a ¼" width, twisting and turning across the fabric. Large-scale prints that have wide areas of background color aren't as suitable for vines, but many large-scale prints with very little background space provide wonderful opportunities.

Large-scale print

Large-scale print with green and other colors to show possible leaf and petal cuts

When fabric hunting, look for overall prints in which the color changes quickly. The more quickly the color changes, the more versatile the fabric. These fabrics often have a watercolor or diffused appearance. The pattern is not as easily recognized as most large-scale prints; since it is soft-edged it reads as nonrepresentational when selectively cut.

Large-scale overall print with indistinct pattern

Medium-scale overall print

Solids are always reliable for appliqué, but to create texture, use small overall or tone-on-tone prints instead. These fabrics will read as solids, but adding the print creates the right amount of texture for any stem, leaf, or petal. Use a set of gradated solids for the precise effect needed in an area requiring a value change. Due to the layering process there will be very little quilting within each flower; to prevent a loss of texture and dimension, avoid using solids of the same color and value next to each other.

Tone-on-tone prints

Don't forget to include plaids, stripes, and other geometric prints in your fabric choices. Use them exclusively to create a folk-art/primitive look. Sprinkled in with other fabrics, they add a surprise texture to any block.

Small-scale prints

If you become frustrated when choosing fabrics for any particular block, put the block aside, have a snack, and forget about the problem. Everything will look fresh when you return to the work, and usually the solution to your dilemma is right at your fingertips. Remember, there's no time limit for completing blocks—appliqué is not a competitive sport. It is, however, for your pleasure. Keep it fun and you will produce more work.

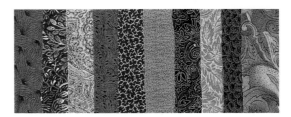

Gradated solids

Finally, with color and fabric, give yourself permission to do anything. Don't "overthink" or become obsessive about each block. Overthinking never made anything better, but it does make everything take longer.

Plaids, Geometrics, Stripes

One at a Time or All at Once

One of the questions that I am most often asked about color and fabrics is "How do you work—do you choose all the fabrics for the entire quilt before beginning or select fabrics for each block individually as you come to it?" There is no right or wrong answer to this question. Quiltmakers work the way in which they feel most comfortable. Choosing a background fabric is a necessity before beginning any appliqué project, but everything else is up for grabs.

Instead of choosing a complete palette for the quilt, try selecting a palette for each block. Start with the primary or "focus" flower. If the focus flower is orange, adding a little purple somewhere in the block creates sparkle. Purple, green, and orange form a triad on the color wheel; so do their variations: lavender, lime green, peach—the list goes on. Allow the focus flower to be your guide for all the other elements.

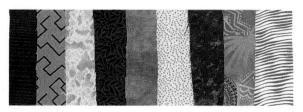

Purple, green, orange

For a more cohesive look to the quilt, choose one or two fabrics to include in each block. These repeated fabrics add unity to the floral appliqué project just as they do in a scrap quilt project.

Leaf fabrics are a good choice for repeating since each block has a variety of leaf sizes and shapes for the eye to follow. However, don't feel that repeating fabrics is necessary to unify the quilt. Fabric colors flow together in floral appliqué as colors do in nature, so the viewer's eye sees the color groups as unified.

Each quiltmaker has a personal color aesthetic that guides the choices she makes. Trust your inner vision when choosing the fabrics for these blocks. If you feel unsure of any choice, let this feeling guide you. There may be a simple change that will make a big difference in the finished look of the block.

Choosing fabrics in a block-by-block fashion adds a large variety of fabrics to the project and increases the visual interest of the quilt. This method can help keep you excited about the work when each element is a new fabric or a new color. No matter how you decide to work, play freely with the fabrics and colors before making a decision.

The Washday Blues or Reds

To prewash or not to prewash—that is the question. To be honest, this was never a question in the past. Everyone went directly to the washer with new fabrics before adding them to the stash. Within the past few years, zealous members on both sides have fueled the controversy over prewashing fabrics. You, of course, must decide for yourself, but consider the following arguments.

❧ Prewashing can reduce the risk of exposure to dye and sizing chemicals. These chemicals can cause a variety of reactions, from minor rashes to the major symptoms typical of allergies. For this reason alone, many quiltmakers wash their fabrics.

❧ Fabrics of intense color often contain an excess amount of dye, which can discharge onto other fabrics when any kind of moisture is present. Quilts don't have to be washed to bleed. High humidity can release some fabric dyes. Prewashing helps remove excess dye, preventing future damage to the quilt.

❧ Prewashing can also alert you to any fabrics that have a tendency to discharge dye. Some fabrics have so much excess dye that they are unsuitable for use. A good rule of thumb is to wash more than once any fabric whose dye colors the water. If, after the second wash and rinse, dye is still present in the water, allow the fabric to dry and then rub it against a piece of white fabric. If any of the color rubs off onto the white fabric, consider the colored fabric a risk.

No one wants quilts ruined by fugitive dye. Prewashing takes so little time for the resulting benefits that there seems to be no reason not to do it. There are, however, some polished cottons that lose their sheen when washed. If this sheen is important to you, don't wash the fabric before using it, but be aware of the risks and trade-offs you are making.

To be safe, prewash all your fabrics. Keep a stacking bin or a small basket in the laundry room or the studio for new, unwashed fabrics. This alleviates any confusion about what is or isn't washed. Whether you use the washer or sink to prewash, use warm water and a small amount of detergent if desired. The fabric isn't dirty so it doesn't need cleaning, but a small amount of detergent aids in the removal of sizing and releases the excess dye. When the washing is done, dry your fabrics by either putting them through a regular dryer cycle or allowing them to air dry. If you remove your fabrics from the dryer before they are completely dry, they will be less wrinkled. Any wrinkles that are present will easily press out.

Background Fabric as a Design Element

Fabric is the quiltmaker's paint; the needle and thread, the brush. The first layer of a painting is the background. This is also true for appliqué. Often we don't consider the background fabric as an integral part of the design. It becomes merely a foundation for the elements on the surface. In contemporary floral appliqué, the background fabric is expanded to an element of the design.

Small overall print

The choice of background fabric (or fabrics) creates an atmosphere for the quilt—Oriental, Art Deco, or Victorian. Pieced backgrounds can create a sky/horizon look. While choosing background fabrics, the first guideline is to look for a texture or design that doesn't detract from the flowers themselves. The right or front side of fabric often has too much color or pattern. Check to see if the back side of the same fabric is subtle enough to make it usable as a background fabric.

Back side of above print

Changing background fabrics within the same quilt also provides more visual interest to your work. Many of the quilts pictured in this book include different fabrics in each of the component blocks. One example of this is shown in my quilt "In Bloom," shown on page 36. Two fabrics of the same print but in different colors, used with a third fabric, work quite effectively.

Coordinate three workable background fabrics for each project. Using several fabrics is the foundation of background as a design element. One approach is to choose one fabric for the feature blocks (those blocks providing a focal point for the quilt), a second fabric for the complementary blocks (those blocks supporting the feature blocks), and a third fabric for the spacers (those blocks added to "fill in" spaces left when placing the feature and complementary blocks).

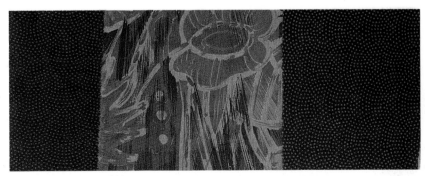
Coordinated background fabrics

If you wish to work in fewer fabrics, use the front and back sides of one fabric for the feature blocks and borders. Add a second fabric for the setting strips or sashing. See the spectacular success of this effect in "Rosehurst—Christine's English Garden," shown on page 40.

Technical considerations can affect background fabric choices. These multilayered blocks can become quite heavy with thread and fabrics; experience has taught me that muslin as a background fabric doesn't support this much weight successfully. Another consideration involves the use of reverse appliqué within the blocks for stems and vines. Successful reverse appliqué demands a tight, closely woven thread to prevent excess fraying of the seam allowances. Keep this in mind if you plan to include reverse appliqué in your work.

Use color and value to your advantage in background fabrics. Dark background fabrics brighten any fabric placed on them, lighter background fabrics soften or tone down any colors used in the flowers, and gray backgrounds show the true color. (Refer to the quilts in the Gallery on pages 36–44.)

Changing colors within the background in Peggy Cord's quilt "Images of Time" shown on page 42, shows the complementary vine block moving through the seasons. Simple but effective, the choice of these three backgrounds emphatically states the maker's intention.

In the quilt "Trellised Flower Garden," shown on page 38, a medium-value background gives the impression that there is a garden of flowers somewhere in the distance behind the feature blocks. The background fabric resembles a watercolor painting, lending an impressionistic feeling to the quilt. Even though this background color is obvious, the diffuse quality of the pattern makes it suitable. This choice offers proof that unusual fabrics are worth considering as background elements. The background fabric is strong in value when standing alone, yet becomes secondary to the pattern when the flowers are applied.

There is no limit to the type of atmosphere you can create with background fabrics. As a first step, give yourself permission to use something other than a solid, light background. Once you have gotten past that, you will never look at background fabrics in the same way. Haunt the fabric bins with nothing but background fabrics in mind. These little excursions can be a budgetary disaster, but they provide an endless source of inspiration for future quilts.

The whole idea is to push the limits of fabrics you would commonly use. The background fabric for the three single-block quilts shown on page 44 has an obvious repeat stripe—so obvious that it would seem distracting. The color changes within the stripe and the printed pattern of the fabric follow that same direction. Turning the fabric so that the stripe runs horizontally, not vertically, weakens the visual effect. After the flowers are applied, the effect of the stripe is negligible. The results are worth the risk.

Stretch the limits of your usual choices. If you see a fabric you want to try for your background but you are unsure of the results, buy enough for one block. Appliqué enough of the block to see what is happening—you haven't lost anything but a little effort. What you may have gained is immeasurable to the visual effect of your quilt.

BEFORE YOU BEGIN

Notions and More

Appliqué requires only the most basic of hand sewing tools. Here are a few tips that should prove valuable when you start sewing.

Needles can make a difference. You might not think that something as simple as a needle could make a difference, but it does. My favorite needle is a size eleven or size twelve sharp. Long enough to aid in the needle-turn process, they are thin and feel comfortable in your hand. They are limber enough to allow you to make small, close stitches, and their thinness prevents them from splitting threads in the fabric. Milliner's needles are also suitable if you can adjust to the extra length.

Quilting needle
(between) ———————
Sharp ———————
Crewel ———————
Milliner's ———————

A shorter needle, such as a between, puts your hand too close to the seam allowance. This can cause the edges of the fabric to fray while turning under the seam allowance.

Thread color for appliqué is important. Always match the thread color to the fabric you are applying, not the background fabric (except when reverse-appliquéing—then match the thread to the background). This will help hide your stitches. If you cannot find the exact color, choose a darker value of the color needed since thread appears lighter when sewn. If an exact match isn't available, gray thread blends with a variety of cool colors, but it doesn't work as well with warm colors.

Any brand of cotton thread is good for appliqué. Look for fifty-weight thread, which is available in a wide variety of colors. Silk thread is good when appliquéing silk fabrics, but it has a tendency to tangle and knot. Cotton thread, the same fiber as the fabric, is therefore the most suitable.

Even the length of thread used can make appliqué easier. Cut the thread 12"–18" long. Shorter lengths such as this prevent tangles and knots and lessen the work of drawing through long thread lengths. Long threads tend to wear thin where they lie against the eye of the needle, causing the thread to split. When this happens, the thread must be changed anyway, so start with a shorter thread and save yourself the trouble.

A good pair of scissors is essential in appliqué. Use two pairs—one for fabric and one for paper. Both should be small, 3"–5" scissors, and sharp to the point. Larger scissors are hard to use when trimming seam allowances or cutting out from behind the appliqué as you layer. Look for a good brand of embroidery scissors for all-purpose appliqué scissors.

Although the techniques described later suggest basting instead of pinning to hold your appliqué in place, you need good-quality silk pins. The pins hold the pieces in place until you finish basting. Select silk pins with as small a diameter as possible. They glide into the fabric easily and never damage the fabric. These pins come in different lengths, with or without glass heads.

Another essential tool is a thimble of some type. Many quiltmakers who don't come from a sewing background find adjusting to a metal thimble difficult. For appliqué, any soft leather or fiber thimble is suitable since the pressure applied during sewing is minimal. When you appliqué, the tendency is to push the needle through at the same spot with the pad or side of the finger. Often a callous develops at this spot, or repeated pushing with the eye of the needle causes continual pricking. The thimble keeps this from happening. If you become accustomed to wearing a "soft" thimble while you appliqué, it may make it easier for you to wear a "regular" thimble for the quilting later.

Gather a large selection of marking pencils since you will not be marking directly on the background fabric. The drawn line in appliqué is the sewing line, so its accuracy is important. If you cannot see the drawn line clearly, you will struggle with your appliqué. Furthermore, if the drawn line is still visible when you finish your appliqué, it will flaw the delicate look of the work.

Any mechanical pencil with a fine lead is a good marking tool for lighter fabrics. Use a silver pencil, kept sharp, for darker fabrics. The secret is to keep the line fine and visible. If you are brave, careful, and promise to turn the drawn line completely under, use what I prefer—the finest point permanent Pigma™ pen in black and brown. Remember, the Pigma pen contains permanent ink, so be careful when marking and sewing. The advantage is a fine, highly visible sewing line. Mark a line on a practice piece to see if you enjoy using it.

Later, on page 28, you will learn a special secret requiring liquid fabric glue. Any brand that dries colorless and prevents fraying works well. Regardless of the brand you choose, test it on your fabrics before using it. Glue can discolor fabrics, so pretesting is essential.

To make the master patterns, use freezer paper, tracing paper, or graph paper. If you choose to work with paper templates, use freezer paper for them, too.

Since you won't be drawing on your background fabric, you will need a light source for pattern placement. Work at a well-lit window or use a glass-top table with a lamp under it as a makeshift light table.

Make your own "light box."

The best investment you can ever make for your appliqué work is a light box or light table. It provides a constant source of light for transferring patterns. I work exclusively with a light table now and enjoy it more and more.

Figuring Yardage

There are no exact yardage requirements since each quilt design varies in the number of blocks and set. Here are some guidelines to aid in calculating the yardage needed. *Remember to add a little extra to allow for shrinkage and trimming edges.*

Feature Blocks

These blocks finish to a 16" x 16" square. Since background fabrics shrink somewhat during appliqué, start with an 18" x 18" square for each feature block. Calculate yardage based on a 42"–44" width from selvage to selvage and cut four of these squares from one yard of fabric. For a four-block quilt, purchase 1⅛ yards. For a twelve-block quilt, purchase 3⅜ yards.

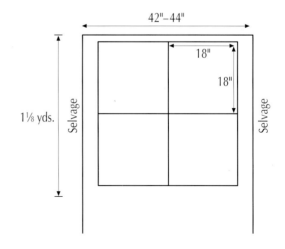

Complementary Blocks

8" x 8" squares   8" x 16" rectangular vine block

These square floral and leaf blocks measure 8" x 8" finished. Cut each background square 10" x 10" for these blocks. If you cut four squares from selvage to the selvage, purchase ⅓ yard. For twelve squares, purchase 1 yard.

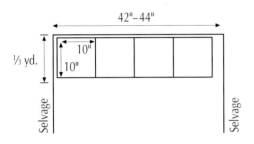

The rectangular vine blocks measure 8" x 16" finished. Cut each background rectangle for these blocks 10" x 18" to allow for any shrinkage during appliqué. Fabric cut with the 18" length parallel to the selvage edge provides four rectangles as shown. Purchase ⅝ yard for four of these complementary blocks. Purchase the same amount of background and vine fabric if you plan reverse appliqué or cutwork for the vine.

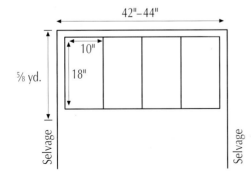

If the pattern of the fabric requires cutting the 10" length parallel to the selvage edge, calculate ⅝ yard of fabric to cut four rectangles measuring 10" x 18". Pur-

chase ⅔ yard for four of these complementary blocks to allow for shrinkage.

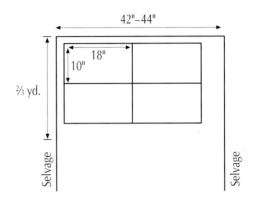

The rectangular vine blocks measure 8" x 16" finished. Cut each background rectangle for these blocks 10" x 18" to allow for any shrinkage during appliqué. Fabric cut with the 18" length parallel to the selvage

Spacers and Borders

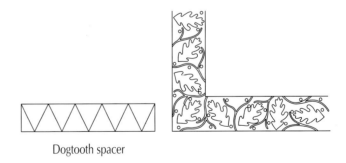

Dogtooth spacer

When calculating yardage for the spacer and border fabrics, add 2" to each finished dimension of each unit. Diagram the block setting you select for your quilt. Include a cutting size for each unit as well as the finished dimensions. Use this diagram to calculate how much of each background fabric you need.

In the diagram below there are four dogtooth strips, each measuring 2" x 16".

Cut these strips 4" x 18" to allow for any shrinkage during appliqué. If cut with the 4" dimension parallel to the selvages, they require ¼ yard. If cut with the 18" dimension parallel to the selvages, they require ½ yard. Round up to the nearest ⅛ yard to allow for errors.

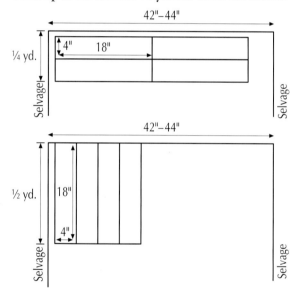

For a full-length appliqué border, calculate the dimensions of the quilt before borders are added and add 2"–4" to each dimension for shrinkage. Cutting the border fabric in widths from selvage to selvage and then piecing the borders to the necessary lengths reduces the amount of fabric needed.

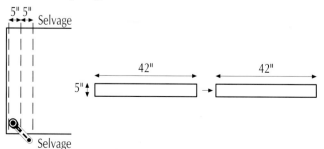

If you choose not to piece your borders, you must buy yardage equal to the length of the quilt plus the allowance for shrinkage.

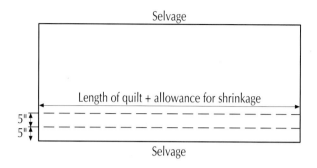

For the dogtooth borders, purchase the same amount of the dogtooth fabric as calculated for the border. If you need 1 yard for borders, purchase the same amount of fabric for the dogtooth. Remember to add 2"–4" for shrinkage.

Appliquéd Cornerstones

The appliquéd cornerstone blocks measure 4" x 4". Cut each background square 6" x 6" for these blocks. All six of these blocks will fit across one width of fabric, 42"–44" wide, from selvage to selvage. Purchase ¼ yard.

Appliqué Pieces

For the appliqué pieces, ¼ yard of each fabric is usually sufficient but ½ yard is playing it safe.

❧ Tip ❧

The only fabric that is necessary to buy all at once is the background fabric. Purchase it in sections, buying all the feature-block background first. Purchase the complementary background later, then the spacer and border fabric if you choose not to purchase it all at once.

PREPARING THE BLOCK

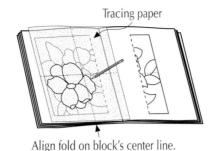
Tracing paper

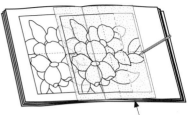

Align fold on block's center line.

Match block edges, then draw remaining block.

Pattern Making

The 16" x 16" feature blocks and the 8" x 16" complementary blocks are drawn full size on the pullout insert pages at the back of the book. If you do not wish to cut apart the pullout page or want to cut paper pieces from the pattern without cutting the original, photocopy or trace the pattern onto paper large enough to include the entire pattern. Before tracing, fold the paper in half first vertically, then horizontally, so that the folds interesect at the center of the block. Match these folds to the center marks on the pattern before tracing. Use these fold lines later for placement on the background block.

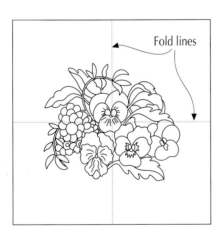
Fold lines

The size of the 8" x 8" blocks prevents the use of a single page for the full-size pattern. Before appliquéing the block, create a master pattern to use for reference.

Start with an 8½" x 11" or larger sheet of tracing paper. Fold the paper in half lengthwise and crosswise. Use the fold lines to match the dotted center lines on the pattern sections. Place the center folds of your graph paper on the appropriate lines and trace the pattern. After finishing one end of the block, match the fold lines and continue tracing the second part of the pattern.

The finished drawing is a permanent pattern. Save it until you are completely finished with your project. Store it, folded in a plastic sleeve, to keep it available indefinitely.

From the background fabric, cut out the block in the size needed. (For cut background block sizes, see "Figuring Yardage" on page 14.) Prepare the background fabric by folding it into halves and quarters and pressing in these folds with a warm iron. These folds will match the paper folds on your pattern for proper placement of the appliqué designs. Use this fabric-folding technique for all the blocks. It provides accurate guidelines for centering the appliqué.

❧ Tip ❧

Mark these center folds additionally by stitching in the fold with a contrasting thread or by marking lightly with a silver pencil. To press out the folds after appliquéing, dampen the fold, then press with a hot iron.

Now you are ready to begin the transfer process. Choose the method by which you will work. To transfer the pattern to the fabric and to place appliqué pieces, I prefer to work at a light box. If you choose this method, complete the master pattern, then tape the drawing to the light box. Use ¼"-wide masking tape, the type used for quilting lines, to secure the pattern to the light box.

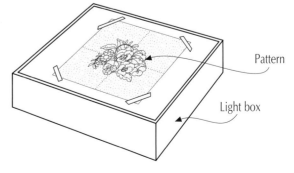
Pattern

Light box

1. Start with piece 1 on the pattern. Choose the fabric for this leaf or flower. With the light box turned on, place the fabric over piece 1. With the marking tool of your choice, trace the exact shape of piece 1 onto the fabric.

2. Cut out the piece, adding a ⅛"-wide seam allowance as you cut. If you are uncomfortable with the narrow (⅛") width or are using fabric that frays easily, cut out the piece, adding wider seam allowances. I prefer the ⅛" seam allowance for more flexibility along curved areas and for less bulk than that created by a wider seam allowance.

3. Place the background fabric over the light box. Place the cut fabric piece on the background fabric, carefully matching the drawn line with the outline drawn on the pattern. Pin in place, baste, and begin your appliqué.

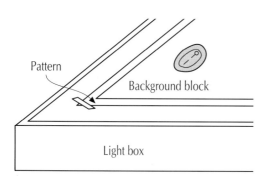

Pattern

Background block

Light box

4. When you finish appliquéing this piece, turn to the back of the block and cut away the background fabric from behind the appliquéd piece, leaving a ¼"-wide seam allowance. (See "Layering," page 22.) Continue to prepare, then appliqué each piece in numerical order until the block is completed.

Templates

Working with a light box and needle-turn appliqué eliminates the need for templates of any kind, decreasing the preparatory time. You may, however, feel more comfortable working with templates. Make either freezer-paper or plastic templates for each element as you come to it. I find freezer paper preferable to plastic because it allows for easier cutting on the most intricate of pieces.

1. Make freezer-paper templates by placing the freezer paper over the pattern, shiny side down, and tracing each piece's exact shape.

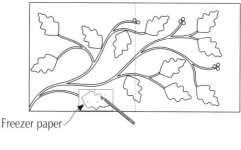

Freezer paper

2. Cut out the traced template but do not add seam allowances.

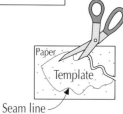

Paper

Template

Seam line

3. Place the freezer-paper piece on the right side of the design fabric, shiny side down. With a dry iron, on the cotton setting, press the freezer-paper template onto the design fabric. When heated, the waxy backing on the paper melts slightly, adhering the template to the fabric.

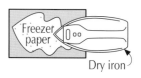

Freezer paper

Dry iron

4. Trace the shape onto the fabric by drawing around the edge of the paper template. Peel off the paper template. Cut out the piece, adding a ⅛"-wide seam allowance, and appliqué in place.

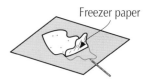

Freezer paper

❧Note❧

For all appliqué, the drawn line is the sewing line, with seam allowances added in the cutting. Never cut on the drawn line; you will not only lose the sewing line, but you will also significantly reduce the size of the appliqué pieces.

❧Tip❧

I don't recommend drawing the appliqué-shape positions onto the background fabric. It is difficult to match or cover these lines. The light box provides the means to see the pattern on the background fabric, making lines drawn on the background superfluous.

Appliqué Techniques

It is hard to believe that at last it is time to appliqué, but here we go!

Basic Needle-Turn Appliqué

There are as many appliqué techniques as there are people who appliqué. If you have perfected a technique, there is no reason to change. If you are a beginner or you still have difficulty with your current technique, try the needle-turn directions that follow. I firmly believe in finding a technique and perfecting it. If you continue to shop for techniques, you may not give yourself the opportunity to "get comfortable" with what you are doing. Whichever method you choose, keep practicing. Don't give up on a technique until you give yourself time to develop it fully.

If you are new to appliqué or your appliqué skills are a little rusty, practice first by following these directions for a needle-turned heart.

1. Using the simple heart template provided, trace the heart pattern onto the uncoated side of a piece of freezer paper. Cut out the heart along the drawn line. Do not add a seam allowance while drawing or cutting the paper template.

Practice Heart Template

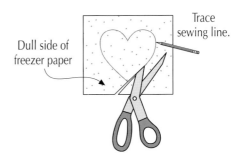

2. With a warm iron, press the coated side of the freezer paper heart onto the right side of the design fabric.

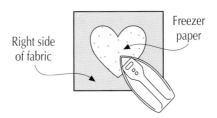

3. Using a marking pencil of your choice, draw around the heart pattern. Lift the freezer paper off the fabric after completing the tracing. The paper template has enough "wax" so that it can be used more than once.

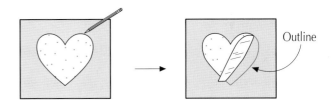

4. Cut a 4" x 4" square of background fabric. Fold the background fabric in half and press, then fold into quarters and press to mark the center. (This is important later when working from the master patterns.) Use the folds as placement lines for the heart.

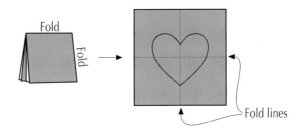

5. Cut out the heart, adding a scant ¼"-wide seam allowance. In most needle-turn appliqué, use as narrow a seam allowance as possible. For more information, turn to the "Troubleshooting" section on pages 22–23.

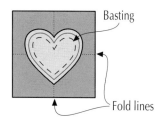

6. Pin the heart to the background fabric, matching the inner point and lower point of the heart with the vertical fold as shown. Leave an equal amount of background fabric above and below the heart. Baste the heart to the background fabric, sewing ½" inside the *drawn* line as shown.

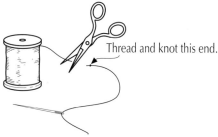

Threading the Needle

Hand stitchers frequently offer lively discussion on how to thread a needle. Which end of the thread is the cut end? What kind of knot should I use? The manufacturer's recommended method for needle threading is to cut a length of thread 12"–18" long from the spool. Thread the newly-cut end through the eye of the needle, pull this end through, and knot it.

When thread is on a spool, knot the end cut from the spool. When thread is in a skein, such as embroidery floss, thread and knot the loose end.

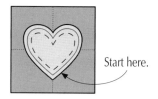

Long staple cotton fibers are "twisted" or spun to create fine cotton thread. Using this technique to thread the

needle and knot the thread keeps the "twist" intact and reduces knotting. It also helps the thread lie in the same direction, aiding in hidden stitches.

The Appliqué Stitch

Now you are ready to appliqué.

1. Start at the straightest line possible, for example, the right side of the heart just above the lower point.

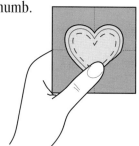

2. Roll the seam allowance under to the drawn line so that the line is hidden. Hold this turned portion in place with your thumb.

3. Bring the needle up from the back side, through both the background fabric and the edge of the fold on the heart. Pretend that you are slipping the needle through the fold created by turning under the seam allowance.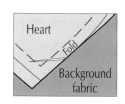

4. Find the spot where the thread came out of the heart. Insert the needle tip slightly behind that thread and into the background as close as you can to the heart without stitching through it.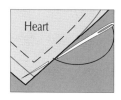

Push the needle forward, bringing the needle tip up through the background and out through the fold line of the heart.

Tip

Keep the needle almost parallel to the heart instead of perpendicular to prevent the stitches from showing. The needle moves toward the hand holding the appliqué. The drawn line and the stitches can be seen better when stitching toward yourself.

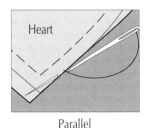 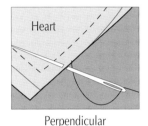

Parallel   Perpendicular

5. Continue, inserting the needle just behind the last point where the thread came out, into the background, and up through the heart. Whenever necessary, stop and use the needle to turn under more of the seam allowance.

Tip

If it feels awkward to use the needle to turn under the seam allowance, try a glass-headed pin or even a toothpick for turning, but don't use your fingers. Turning the seam allowance with fingers can cause the fabric to fray. The moisture in your hands can cause the loose threads to stick to your fingers. In addition, when using fingers for turning, the tendency is to press a finger-width's fold. This fold may be slightly off the drawn line, losing the appliqué's true shape.

6. Stitch to the point of the heart and take the last stitch right at the end of the drawn line. The seam allowance you just turned under fills up the space where the point lies. Place the tips of your scissors under the heart and trim away only the excess seam allowance under the point of the heart, not the seam allowance for the next side.

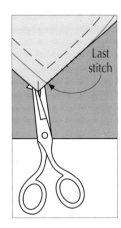

Last stitch

7. Fold the seam allowance under at a right angle to the point. If there is too much seam allowance for the space under the point, trim the underneath portion again.

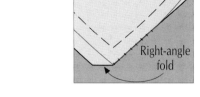

Right-angle fold

8. Take one stitch right in the point and give the thread a gentle tug before starting on the other side of the heart. This should pull the point back into shape if it has been blunted. Roll under the seam allowance to begin stitching and continue to appliqué.

9. At the curve of the heart, slow down. Most of you will be ready to throw something at me for suggesting this, but let me explain. To keep any curve smooth and even, use small, close stitches. If you zoom around the curve with larger stitches, the curve will have little bubbles and bumps. Needle-turn only a small portion of the seam allowance at a time and avoid sewing right to where your thumb is holding the fold. Your thumb can hide any little bumps, so stop before reaching your thumb and turn another portion of the seam allowance.

10. Clip to the inner point when you are close enough to it that the seam allowance no longer turns under the appliqué. To prevent fraying, never clip into the "inny" until you reach it. Cut right to the point on the line, not through it.

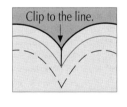

Clip to the line.

11. Turn under the remaining seam allowance all the way to this cut. Appliqué to the center. Take a single stitch exactly at the point. Turn under the seam allowance on the other side of the point and continue to appliqué the remaining curve.

12. The center stitches in the inner point should create an inverted V, with one stitch on the right of the point, one in the point itself, and the last stitch to the left of the point.

13. Continue to appliqué until reaching the spot where you started. Take a few stitches beyond the first stitch.

14. Push the needle through to the back. Take a small "bite" of fabric ⅛" away from the stitching line and tie a knot. This keeps the knot from showing through the background fabric.

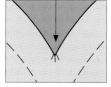

Stitches form inverted "V".

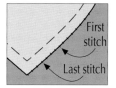

First stitch

Last stitch

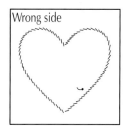

Wrong side

End stitching ⅛" away from edge.

Concave Curves

A concave curve is the only shape in appliqué that isn't found on the practice heart. Concave curves can be gentle S-curves or sharp dips. On the gentle S-curves, small seam allowances are usually sufficient to aid in turning. If that doesn't help, clip along the curve to the drawn line (but not through the line) to release the fabric so that it needle-turns easily.

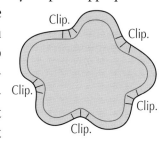

Clip.

On a sharp concave curve, it is necessary to clip to the drawn line in at least three places to release the seam allowance. After clipping to the line, needle-turn the entire curve for a smooth line. The more acute the curve, the more clipping may be required. Try to leave some space between clips—⅛" when possible. Look for the position where the curve starts and where it is the most acute to make your cuts.

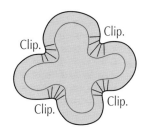

Clip.

Layering

The floral motifs in the blocks in this book are multi-layered, with focus flowers falling on top of background leaves and flowers. Layering occurs in much of appliqué. Keep multilayered appliqué blocks flat and smooth by cutting away the background behind each piece after appliquéing it.

Cutting out from behind means simply cutting away the background fabric beneath the appliquéd piece, leaving a ¼"-wide seam allowance.

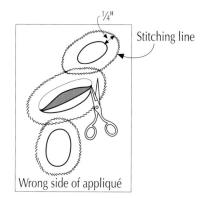

¼"

Stitching line

Wrong side of appliqué

This releases the background fabric so that the block will lie flatter. It also reduces the bulk and weight of the fabric by removing one layer. When you trim away part of a previously appliquéd piece, remember not to cut through the sewn line unless you can in some way reinforce that stitching.

Another reason to cut away the background fabric after appliquéing is to see through the fabric when using a light box. (See page 14.) Multiple layers will not allow the light to pass through the block.

Troubleshooting

If you encounter any problems doing needle-turn appliqué, refer to the following for possible solutions.

Problem 1. My stitches show.

- Make sure the thread color matches the color of the heart fabric.
- Make sure the thread isn't going into the background fabric too far away from the heart or coming out too far inside the heart as you stitch.

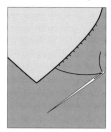
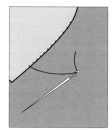

❧ Your needle is moving perpendicular to the fold, not parallel to the fold. (See page 21.)

❧ Your tension is too loose; pull the thread a little tighter.

Problem 2. The drawn line is showing.

❧ Roll the seam allowance farther under the heart, completely hiding the drawn line.

❧ Decrease the size of your seam allowance in order to fit the entire line under the heart.

Problem 3. My curves are bumpy, not smooth.

❧ You are using too much seam allowance. Too much fabric in the seam allowance creates bulk along a curve. Trim down the seam allowance to ⅛" and try again.

❧ Your stitches are too large or far apart. Try smaller, more closely spaced stitches.

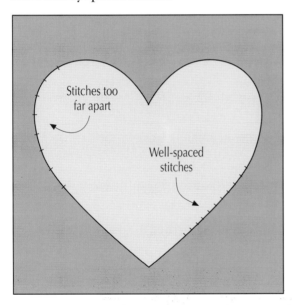

Stitches too far apart

Well-spaced stitches

❧ Your tension is too loose. Pull the thread a little tighter as you stitch. My grandmother taught me a trick for hand-sewing tension. She said if you always draw the thread through with your little finger, the tension will be perfect for hand sewing. Using the wrist to pull the thread through causes tension to be either too tight or too loose.

Problem 4. My points aren't sharp.

❧ Trim away excess seam allowance. Excess seam allowance at the point creates a bulge.

❧ Remember to gently tug on the stitch taken right at the point to pull it back into shape.

Problem 5. My appliqué is loose and pulls away from the background.

❧ Your tension is too loose. It is better to pull the thread a little too tight and correct it while pressing than to make the stitching too loose and risk an appliquéd piece coming off. (See the note about tension in Problem 3.)

Problem 6. My fabric keeps fraying in the inner point.

❧ Try "painting" a little liquid fabric glue on the outside of the drawn line. Use the point of a silk pin as your brush. Allow the glue to dry before continuing to appliqué. Be careful not to get any glue inside the drawn line, as it may show on the finished piece.

Some fabric glue discolors, so be sure to test it on your fabric. Since the glue is liquid and may leak through to the background, paint the glue to the appliqué piece before basting the piece into place. If the piece is already basted into place, slip an index card under the appliqué piece so that the glue won't accidentally bleed onto the background fabric. Allow the glue to dry before removing the index card.

Fabric glue

ADDITIONAL TECHNIQUES

Several techniques used in contemporary floral appliqué will probably be familiar to you. Many are used in new ways or are used to achieve special effects. For easy reference, read the list of suggestions accompanying each pattern. Refer to the following technical descriptions for basic information.

Stems

Reverse Appliqué

Accomplish small, delicate stems with greater ease using reverse appliqué. Consider first your background fabric. Any tightly woven cotton works well for reverse appliqué. Loosely woven fabrics or fabrics woven from fat threads are more difficult, if not impossible, to reverse appliqué successfully.

Reverse appliqué is useful in any appliqué project to create added dimension. In direct appliqué, each piece lies on top of the background fabric, bringing the work toward the viewer. In reverse appliqué, the design fabric lies under the background fabric, creating the illusion of that piece moving away from the viewer. Reverse appliqué becomes a part of the surface, not an addition to the surface.

1. Begin by drawing the stem pattern onto the right side of the background fabric. Reverse appliqué is the only time you draw directly on the background fabric.

2. Cut a piece of design (vine) fabric large enough to extend entirely under the stem. Pin the design fabric into place behind the background fabric, right sides up.

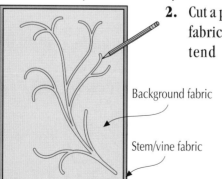

Background fabric

Stem/vine fabric

3. Baste ⅛"–¼" outside the drawn line. Cut inside the channel created by the drawn lines. Be sure to cut along the center of the channel so you have enough seam allowance to turn. Avoid cutting the entire length of the vine all at once; cut a few inches at a time, then appliqué, to provide more stability and to prevent fraying. Cut and roll until you have completed one side of the stem or vine.

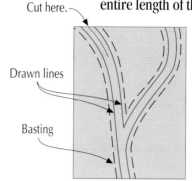

Cut here.

Drawn lines

Basting

4. Roll under and appliqué the opposite side of the stem or vine.

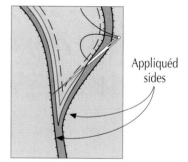

Appliquéd sides

≈Tip≈

Create even tinier stems by drawing a single line for the stem instead of a channel. Baste no more than ⅛" away from the drawn line. This prevents turning under an excessively large seam allowance to maintain the "skinny" stem. Carefully cut along the drawn line, roll under the seam allowance, and begin to appliqué. Appliqué one side of the stem completely before appliquéing the other side.

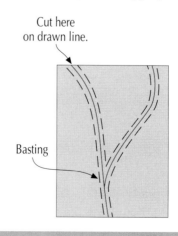

Cut here on drawn line.

Basting

5. Finish the line of stitching for reverse appliqué the same way you would for direct appliqué. Remove the excess stem fabric by cutting it away from the stitching, leaving a ¼"-wide seam allowance. Do not cut on the stitching. Removing this excess fabric prevents any fabric lying under the background fabric from showing through to the front. It also removes an extra fabric layer that creates bulkiness and hinders fine hand quilting.

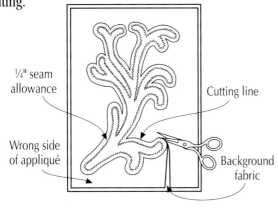

¼" seam allowance

Cutting line

Wrong side of appliqué

Background fabric

Cutwork Appliqué

Cutwork appliqué also works for the vines in the complementary blocks or the oak leaf border. This technique is similar to reverse appliqué.

1. Begin with a piece of design (stem) fabric that is the same size as the background to which it will be applied. Draw the pattern onto the right side of the design fabric. Pin the design fabric on top of the background, right sides up.

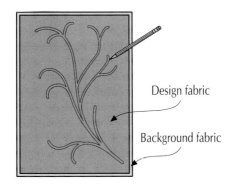

Design fabric

Background fabric

2. Baste inside the drawn line. Cut a ⅛"-wide seam allowance to the outside of the drawn line and begin your appliqué. There often isn't much space for seam

allowances on very narrow vines, so use as narrow a seam allowance as possible.

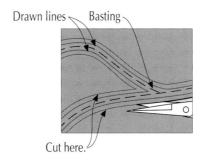

Drawn lines   Basting

Cut here.

3. After cutting, turn the appliqué so you work toward yourself. As you continue to appliqué, pin the excess design fabric out of the way. (This fabric falls completely away from the piece upon completion of the appliqué. Be sure to save this fabric for use in other places.)

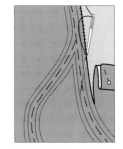

Cut-to-Shape Appliqué

Try cutting many of the stems or vines as pieces specific to their finished shape. Stems cut in this manner can be made smaller than those created by using bias tubes and require very little preparatory work.

1. Trace the exact shape of the stem onto the right side of the design fabric.

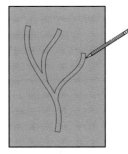

2. Cut out the stem, adding a ⅛"- to ¼"-wide seam allowance.

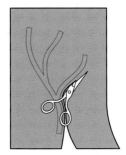

3. Pin the stem to the background fabric and baste inside the drawn line.

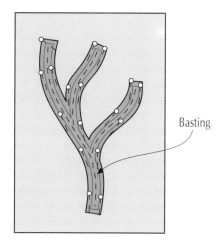

Basting

Tip

Even if the stem isn't a curved shape, cut the shape out on the bias of the fabric so that it lies flat when appliquéd. Often, small stems cut on the straight of grain pucker or pull when appliquéd. Cutting these shapes on the bias eliminates this problem.

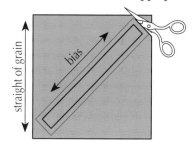

straight of grain

bias

4. Appliqué one side of the stem; remove the basting. Fold back the stem to reveal the seam allowance inside the stem. Trim seam allowance as small as possible.

Wrong side of stem

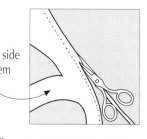

5. Return stem to its proper position; baste again.

Baste again.

6. Complete the appliqué.

Tip

Cutting away the inside seam allowance makes room for the other side of the stem, so you can create tiny, tiny stems. Occasionally, the stem is so small that basting in the channel between the stem lines prevents turning under the seam allowance. When this occurs, before beginning to appliqué, baste along the seam allowance opposite the first seam sewn.

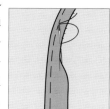

On very narrow stems, no rebasting is required. The appliquéd side will hold the shape in place.

On each block, try to use a combination of these techniques. Each creates a different dimensional look, adding variety and interest to the total effect of the block.

Berries and Blossoms

Detail...detail...detail...it's what separates fine appliqué work from the mediocre. The patterns in contemporary floral appliqué are full of detail. Small flowers with tiny centers, diminutive berries tossed among the flowers—the effect on the finished product is worth all the effort. Add berries any time to any pattern for a special touch (or to cover some pesky mistakes).

Small circles work well for these details, but they aren't always the shape found in nature. The blocks in this book include natural shapes for these details, combined with the "old faithful" circle.

Circles

Okay, I make berries the old-fashioned way—by paper piecing. We'll get to that in a minute, but for now, take note of all the berries on the pyracantha branch in Pattern 9, Roses and Daisies, on page 54. Every one of those little berries was needle-turned. In nature, nothing is perfectly round. Some berries are ovals, flat and elliptical, and some are round but slightly misshapen.

If you prefer, you can needle-turn circles for a more natural effect in the same manner as ovals, by turning and stitching, turning and stitching. If you desire perfectly round berries (and I do love that look), here goes.

1. Using a circle template or any circular object that is the desired size, draw the finished-size berry circle onto an unlined index card. Now cut out the circles on the drawn line. Do not add seam allowances.

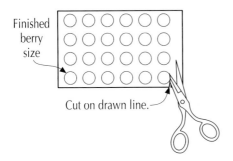

Finished berry size

Cut on drawn line.

2. Cut out fabric circles for each berry template, adding a ¼"-wide seam allowance. With a single thread, knotted at the end, sew a line of small running stitches just inside the cut edge of the right side of the fabric circle.

Wrong side of fabric

Paper piece

3. Place the paper circle inside the fabric circle and gather up the running stitches for perfect circles every time.

Paper piece

❧ Tip ❧

If small bumps appear on the edge of the circle, turn the "berry" to the back side. Take a small stitch in one bump, then take another small stitch on the other side of the circle. Weave your thread back and forth in this manner to remove the bumps.

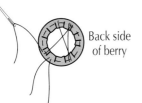

Back side of berry

4. Knot the thread and you are ready to apply the berry. Pin in place—the index card is difficult to baste through—and appliqué the folded edge as you would a needle-turned edge.

Removing Index Cards

You're probably wondering what to do with the index card inside the berry. If the berry is smaller than 1" in diameter, leave the index card inside the berry. Smaller berries don't provide enough seam allowance to risk cutting out from behind the berry to remove the index card. Remove the index card from larger circles to prevent bulk and stiffness.

1. After appliquéing circles with a diameter of 1" or larger, turn the appliqué block over and make a small slit in the center of the background fabric under the circle. Insert the scissor tips in the slit and trim away the background fabric, leaving a ¼"-wide seam allowance.

2. With a small pair of tweezers, pull out the index card. If you have woven threads across the back of the berry, carefully clip the threads before removing the index card.

¼"-wide seam allowance

Back side of fabric

❧ Tip ❧

Office supply or quick print shops are an excellent source of unlined card stock, available in 8½" x 11" sheets for a few cents per sheet.

Ovals

Nature abhors a straight line—and they aren't so easy to appliqué either! Give me a soft curve any day. Are ovals such soft curves? They can be.

It may be hard to believe, but many ovals have a straight line just as the practice heart did—on each side of the oval. Start your appliqué just below the top curve as shown.

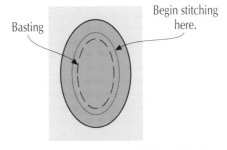

Basting

Begin stitching here.

As you appliqué the oval, turn a small portion of the seam allowance at a time, stitch that section, and turn a little more. The key is to turn and stitch, turn and stitch. As with all other techniques, the narrowest seam allowances make the smoothest curves possible. Don't forget to take the small, close stitches necessary to keep those bumps at bay.

Small ovals, such as those found in the pansy centers in Pattern 1, Pansies and Primroses (page 46), are occasionally so small that there is no room for basting stitches. Try using a small dot of fabric paste (or water-soluble glue stick) to keep the center in place for appliquéing. For larger pieces, basting is the only safe way to secure an appliqué and keep it from shifting positions.

I prefer basting to pinning appliqué pieces in place. Yes, the basting requires more time, but it's well worth it. Often appliqué pieces bunch up or don't lie flat. Basting eliminates this problem. With basting, you never have to worry about threads getting caught in the pins while sewing. Baste several sections at a time and transport your work without worrying about the pieces slipping out of place.

Organic Shapes

Many of the flower centers are star-shaped or of odd organic shapes. They add a more natural look to the flowers, keeping the work visually exciting. For the star shapes or any small shape with sharp points, paint the inside notches of the seam allowances, just outside the drawn line, with a liquid fabric glue before applying the piece. This adds stability to the narrow seam allowances and aids in keeping the small points sharp.

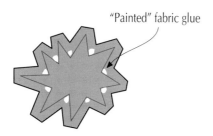

"Painted" fabric glue

Appliqué any small organic shape, such as the iris beard, more easily by painting fabric glue in the seam allowance. Don't become dependent on this technique for all appliqué, but in the right places it can reduce the frustration level.

PRECONSTRUCTION

In general, when appliquéing, prepare as much as possible ahead of time. (It reminds me of cooking for a crowd.) "Building before applying," or preconstruction, is one of my favorite floral-appliqué techniques. Watch for this technique in the numbered instructions given with each pattern. Simply put, it means appliquéing vein lines, flower centers, and other details onto an individual petal or leaf before appliquéing that shape to the block.

Veins, Flower and Leaf Centers

For many of the patterns, you will reverse-appliqué the vein lines to the leaf or petal first, then cut out the leaf and appliqué it to the block. Many of the flowers' centers begin with this technique.

Let's go through, step by step.

1. Draw the leaf shape onto the design fabric, including the vein line. Cut out the leaf, adding a ⅛" to ¼" seam allowance.

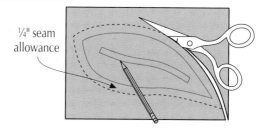

¼" seam allowance

2. Baste the leaf to a square of the fabric that you have chosen for the vein. Be sure to baste outside the drawn line for reverse appliqué. Cut inside the channel created by the drawn line and begin your reverse appliqué. (See "Reverse Appliqué" on page 24.)

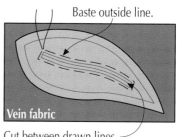

Baste outside line.

Vein fabric

Cut between drawn lines.

3. When finished, turn the fabric over and cut away the vein fabric, leaving a ¼"-wide seam allowance. Place the leaf in position on the block and appliqué.

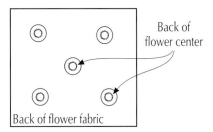

In the patterns, an unnumbered flower piece refers to a piece that is constructed before being applied to the block. For example, the centers of the small flowers to the right of the lotus blossom in Pattern 2, Lotus Blossom and Grapes, should be constructed before appliquéing the flowers. The centers of the flowers on the vine in Pattern 11, Anemones and Anthurium, should be reverse-appliquéd before the flowers are appliquéd to the block. These small centers go even faster if you do several at a time.

1. Draw the blossoms on the design fabric, leaving enough space between the blossoms for a seam allowance. Using a piece of fabric the same size as the blossom fabric, pin the fabrics together as for reverse appliqué, right sides up. Baste on the outside of the drawn lines of the centers.

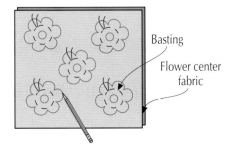

Basting

Flower center fabric

2. Cut a horizontal and vertical line through the center, and if necessary, make a single additional cut between the original cuts.

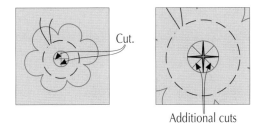

Cut.

Additional cuts

3. Turn and stitch to reverse-appliqué the flower center. When you finish, remove basting, and turn the piece over. From the back, cut away the excess flower center fabric, leaving a ¼"-wide seam allowance.

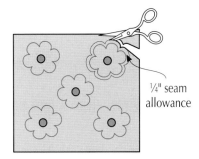

Back of flower center

Back of flower fabric

4. Cut out each flower, remembering to add a ¼"-wide seam allowance.

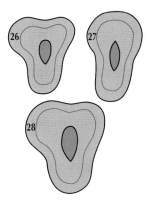

¼" seam allowance

Some flower petals have tiny areas of reverse appliqué. Prepare the petals as you did for steps 1–3 for flower centers. When finished with the reverse appliqué, cut out each petal and set into place for appliquéing. To identify petals for placement, write the number of each petal in the seam allowance.

The peperomia leaves in Pattern 6, Petunias and Sweet Peas, are perfect leaves to build before appliquéing. In any appliqué pattern, look for the opportunity to try this technique.

Turned Leaves and Petals

The turned-leaf technique is an approach to designing that splits a leaf into two or more parts. This split may represent the underside of the leaf turning up and over the top side of the leaf, or it may designate light catching a fold in the center of the leaf, creating a value change.

Fabric use is important for these leaves. Using medium and light values is essential when depicting three-dimensional leaves or petals. In Pattern 1, Pansies and Primroses, the leaves behind the pansies are a good example of split leaves.

Turned leaves and petals appear throughout these patterns. The iris leaves and petals in Pattern 4, Iris and Fuchsias, display just how effective this design technique can be by showing both the inner and outer portion of the leaf or petal.

Follow the numerical sequence of the leaf sections to make appliqué easier and to better achieve the illusion of three-dimensionality. Preconstructing the turned leaves and petals also works well.

FINISHING THE BLOCK

Stippling

Stippling, a pen-and-ink technique, is one of the most widely used techniques for the blocks in this book. It is done with Pigma™ pens, a permanent ink pen available in a variety of colors and point sizes. The stippling is done for shading and adding dimension to the flowers and leaves.

Stipple after the flower or leaf is completely appliquéd, so that the shading can be done more accurately. Start by putting small dots along the edges of the petals or leaves. Occasionally, this creates enough dimension to bring the flowers or leaves into focus. Additional shading can be added where each element meets the next, like a shadow falling onto one leaf or flower from another.

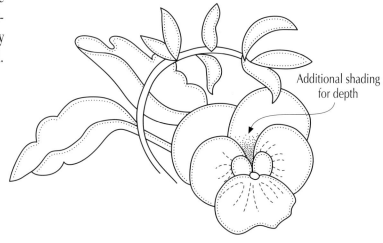

Additional shading for depth

The shading in the rose below (from Pattern 9, Roses and Daisies) creates the illusion that a light source is shining on the rose from above it.

Trace the individual flower onto a sheet of paper, then play with the shading, using a pencil. Where the shadows fall, sketch in the shading. Shade and erase until you are pleased with the dimension created. Refer to this drawing when stippling the appliquéd pieces. When you are finished stippling, heat-set the Pigma ink with a dry iron.

Each oak leaf in the border for "In Bloom" (page 36) was stippled along the outer edges and inside the leaves for shading. I thought the effect would be minimal against the dark background, but it made a visible difference.

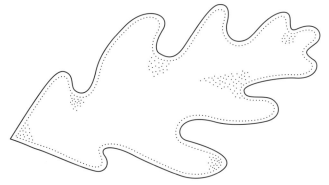

Stippling is not done in the place of embroidery but for an entirely different effect. Stippling becomes part of the surface. Embroidery sits on top of the surface, adding dimension and texture that is closer to the viewer.

Practice stippling before using it on your finished appliqué. Don't be afraid—those who finally find courage to stipple are surprised at how easy it is to do. It is, after all, just one dot after the other, closer together for darker shading, farther apart for lighter shading. What a great addition to your technical bag of tricks!

Squaring Up

After completing all the component blocks, square up each block before constructing the quilt. Carefully press each block, spacer, or border before cutting to the proper size. Remember, feature blocks are 16" x 16" finished (16½" x 16½" cut), and complementary blocks are 8" x 8" (8½" x 8½" cut) or 8" x 16" finished (8½" x 16½" cut). You may need to change the dimensions slightly for your quilt.

A ruler, 16½" x 16½", is perfect for squaring up the blocks. Find the center of the ruler and place it over the center of the block. Align the ruler so that the design portion of the appliqué fits attractively within the finished dimensions. Mark the cutting lines, remove the ruler, and visually check where the design falls before cutting. If the placement fills the space evenly, cut the block along the marked lines.

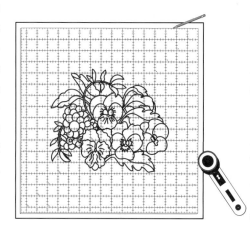

Keep the grain lines in mind when squaring up. To prevent puckering and stretching during construction, avoid any bias edges.

❧ Tip ❧

If you can't find a 16½" x 16½" ruler, make a template from plastic with center lines marked for squaring up. Using the same technique, make templates for the 8½" x 8½" and 8½" x 16½" blocks.

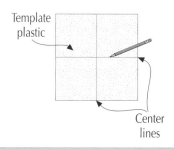

Template plastic

Center lines

ASSEMBLING THE QUILT

On-Point Sets

Blocks that are set together on point require side setting triangles at the ends of the rows. An easy way to cut these triangles is to cut a square in half twice diagonally. Cutting the triangles this way ensures that the straight of grain runs along the long sides of the triangles and along the outside edges of the quilt.

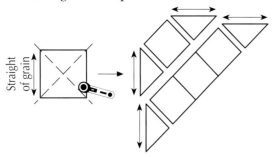

To calculate the size of the square to cut, multiply the finished side of the block by 1.414 to find the diagonal measurement of the block. Add 3" to that measurement to add enough extra to trim after setting the triangles into the quilt. For example, if the on-point block's finished dimensions are 10" x 10", multiply 10" by 1.414 to get 14.14" or (rounding up) 14¼". Add 3" and cut the square 17¼" x 17¼", then cut it in half twice diagonally for 4 side triangles. To cut larger triangles, multiply by 1.5 instead of 1.414, then add 3".

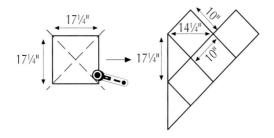

For corner triangles, cut 2 squares in half once diagonally and sew the long sides of the triangles to the quilt. The short sides of the triangles will keep the grain line stable for the quilt's corners.

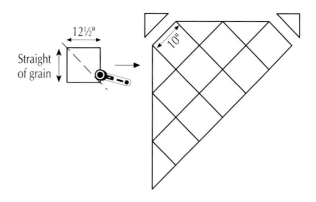

To calculate the size of the square to cut, add 2½" to the block's finished dimension. Cut the square to this size, then cut in half once diagonally. For a 10" finished block, cut a square 12½" x 12½". Cut the square into 2 triangles and sew them to the quilt.

After sewing the side and corner triangles to the quilt, trim away the excess along the outside edge, leaving a ¼"-wide seam allowance.

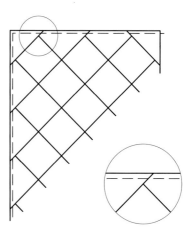

Sashing

For a more traditional setting, try sashing with or without cornerstones. (See "Sashing with Cornerstones" below.) The width of the sashing should complement the scale of the blocks. If you are using printed fabric, the scale of the print shouldn't compete with the scale of the floral appliqué.

A good size for the feature blocks alone is 4"-wide sashing, although a narrower width, from 2"–3" finished, is also attractive. Choose a fabric that coordinates, bringing all the color elements into focus.

The dogtooth spacers in any variation can also be used as sashing in a more traditional set. Combined with the appliquéd cornerstones, these dogtooth sashings are the perfect finishing touch for an appliqué quilt.

1. Cut sashing strips to equal the length of the block.

2. Sew a sashing strip to the right side of each block as shown.

3. Sew sashed blocks together into rows.

4. Sew a sashing strip to the left side of the row.

Note

You may wish to wait until the blocks are sewn together to add the outer sashing strips as you would add a border. In this case, do not sew sashing strips to the blocks along the left and right sides of the quilt before joining them in rows; the sashing on each side will be added as a border after the rows are sewn together.

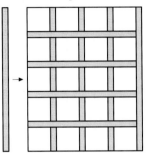

5. Cut horizontal sashing strips the same width as the vertical sashing strips.

6. Sew horizontal sashing strips between rows of blocks. Add the top and bottom sashing strips last.

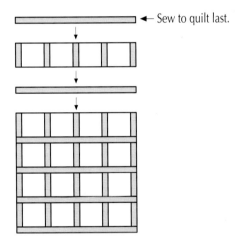

← Sew to quilt last.

Sashing with Cornerstones

Cornerstones are squares added where the sashing intersects. Their dimensions equal the width of the sashing strips.

1. Sew sashing strips to the blocks, following steps 1–3 for sashing without cornerstones.

2. Cut horizontal sashing strips the same dimensions as the sashing strips in step 1.

3. Sew a cornerstone to one end of each sashing strip as shown.

4. Join sashing strips as shown, then sew a cornerstone to the left end of the strip.

5. Sew a sashing unit to each block unit as shown. Take care to match the seam lines of the cornerstones to the seam lines of the vertical sashing strips.

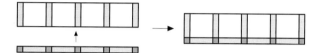

Borders

Borders on quilts serve to frame the main body of the quilt. A border can be pieced, appliquéd, or cut from a single strip of fabric. Adding several complex borders gives importance to the work at the center of the quilt, but take care that the borders do not become more important than the work they are framing! A complex quilt may benefit from the simplicity of a single border, giving the eye a rest from the intricate work in the quilt's center.

When cutting strips for borders, you must decide whether to use straight-cut corner borders or borders with mitered corners.

In either case, if you plan to cut the border strips along the lengthwise grain, that is, parallel to the selvages of the fabric, purchase enough fabric so that you will not need to piece the borders. Cut the borders on grain for less stretch—important if you are sewing borders to bias edges or an on-point set.

If the sides of your quilt measure more than 40" and you don't mind the look of pieced borders, cut your borders across the width of the fabric, from selvage to selvage. You may need to cut several strips and join them end to end to fit your quilt, but since they use less fabric, they are more economical than using unpieced border strips cut lengthwise.

❧Note❧

On appliquéd borders, the piecing lines are often hidden by the appliqué shapes, so the appearance is the same as seamless lengthwise strips. Usually the quilting lines will also conceal any piecing lines.

Borders with Straight-Cut Corners

1. Measure through the center of the quilt top from side to side. Cut border strips, sew them together if necessary to make them long enough, then cut them equal to the measurement of the quilt. It is important to cut the border strips to this measurement. If the edges of the quilt have stretched, or if one side is a little shorter than the other, this center measurement will provide a consistent length across the quilt and will prevent wavy borders on the quilt.

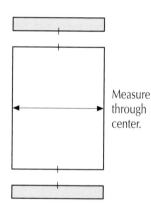

Measure through center.

Mark centers.

2. Mark the center of the quilt and the center of the borders. Mark additional points along the quilt and border if desired. Match markings, pin, then sew the top and bottom borders to the quilt.

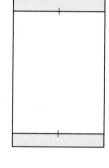

3. Measure through the center of the quilt from top to bottom, including the borders just added. Cut side border strips, join if necessary, and cut to this length. Mark the quilt and border as you did in step 2, then pin and sew borders to each side of the quilt.

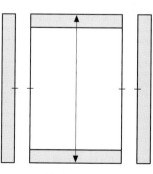

Mark centers.

Borders with Mitered Corners

1. Measure the outer dimensions of the quilt. Cut border strips to this length plus 2 times the border width. Add 2"–3" for seam allowances and a "goof factor." For example a 6"-wide border must be cut the length of the quilt plus 14"–15". If you are planning multiple borders, sew individual border strips together and treat them as one border for mitering instead of sewing them to the quilt one by one.

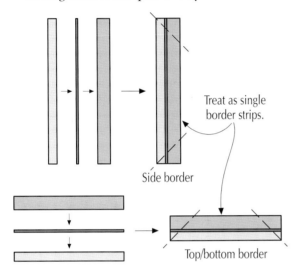

Treat as single border strips.

Side border

Top/bottom border

2. Measure through the quilt from top to bottom and mark this measurement on the border. Mark the center and along the sides of the quilt and border strip. Match markings, pin, then sew each border to the quilt top, starting and stopping the stitching line ¼" from the end of the quilt.

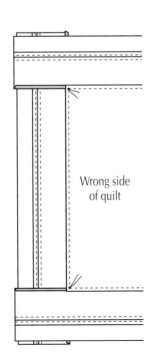

Wrong side of quilt

3. Place the first corner to be mitered on the ironing board, right side up. Pin the quilt as necessary to keep it from shifting. Fold one of the border strips under at a 45° angle and pin in place, matching border seams if necessary. Press.

4. Starting at the outside edge of the quilt, place a piece of masking tape over the fold, removing pins as you center the tape over the fold.

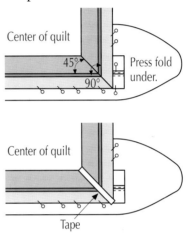

Center of quilt

45°
90°

Press fold under.

Center of quilt

Tape

5. Unpin the quilt from the ironing board and turn it over. Draw a line along the crease formed by the iron. With right sides together, refold the quilt diagonally from the corner, keeping the adjacent border strips together with long edges aligned. Stitch along the pencil line, remove the tape, and check miter for accuracy before trimming the seam allowances to ¼". Press seam allowances open. Repeat for the remaining three corners.

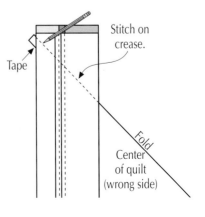

Stitch on crease.

Tape

Fold

Center of quilt (wrong side)

In Bloom by Gabrielle Swain, 1994, Watauga, Texas, 61" x 82". Outstanding color work within the blocks and border joins with representational designs to create realistic flowers in this quilt. The asymmetrical setting, combined with gradated dogtooth spacers and complementary vine blocks work together to draw the viewer's eye to each block.

Kaizen by Linda C. Gillespie, 1994, Plano, Texas, 58" x 69". An asymmetrical border and falling oak leaves, combined with six feature blocks, create an Oriental mood in this stunning quilt. Linda has already won two blue ribbons with "Kaizen."

Trellised Flower Garden by Helen Ruth Brandhurst, 1993, Watauga, Texas, 55" x 75". Light background fabric and a quilted vine for the border give a fresh, springtime look to this quilt. "Trellised Flower Garden" is Helen Ruth's first appliqué quilt.

Garden View by Dee Shaffer, 1994, Texarkana, Texas, 72" x 92". A traditional setting is taken one step further with the addition of appliquéd cornerstones and opulent sashing fabric in this beautiful quilt.

Rosehurst—Christine's English Garden by Ruth Cattles Cottrell, 1994, Irving, Texas, 82" x 99". Batik fabric and appliquéd vines are a lovely addition to this quilt. Ruth used a wide range of color and value within the twelve blocks.

A Gathering of Purple by Marilyn Mowry, 1994, Irving, Texas, 40" x 40". Simple in execution, this quilt uses many fabrics, making it a masterpiece of color. The repetition of this single design with vines shows the effectiveness of individual blocks when used together. For the setting triangles, Marilyn adapted the motifs from the "Vine with Buds and Blossoms" block on page 62.

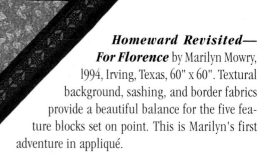

Homeward Revisited— For Florence by Marilyn Mowry, 1994, Irving, Texas, 60" x 60". Textural background, sashing, and border fabrics provide a beautiful balance for the five feature blocks set on point. This is Marilyn's first adventure in appliqué.

Barbara's Bloomin' Birthday by Gabrielle Swain, 1994, Watauga, Texas, 36" x 36". Appliquéd blocks, offset with pieced checkerboard blocks, make this a striking example of how to use just a few blocks to create a smaller quilt.

Images of Time by Peggy Cord, 1994, Garland, Texas, 30" x 36". Seasonally inspired background fabrics and corresponding color changes in vines and leaves make this successful as a year-round design.

La Petite Fleur by Gabrielle Swain, 1994, Watauga, Texas, 50" x 32". Six of the 8" x 8" floral blocks, combined with an asymmetrical floral border, create a delicate quilt, perfect for a beginning appliqué project.

In Hope of Entwives by Susan B. Elliott, 1994, Trophy Club, Texas, 49" x 32". Art Deco in feeling, these four vines were appliquéd entirely by machine with the Smoothstitch™ appliqué technique. The zigzag dogtooth and asymmetrical borders provide a lovely finishing touch.

Fresh Cut Flowers by Gabrielle Swain, 1994, Watauga, Texas, each 16" x 16". Individual blocks quilted, bound, and placed together make a beautiful arrangement in any room. The dramatic background fabric allows these blocks to stand alone.

FEATURE BLOCKS

These floral-arrangement designs include a variety of flowers that may not all be available in the same season. For me, part of the fun in designing was being able to choose flowers that felt right together, stretching nature's boundaries. Occasionally, flowers and/or leaves float, unattached to stems, to alleviate confusion and weight. Combining many leaf shapes creates more visual interest, although they may not be the "proper" leaf for the flower.

If a block looks daunting, remember, no matter how complex the pattern appears overall, it is completed by finishing one single element at a time. All of the smaller elements, plus the large focus flower, ground leaves, or blossoms, work together to create the complexity of the arrangement. There is only one restriction: you must follow the numbered sequence so that all the elements will fall into place correctly. Multilayered appliqué is simple in execution, complex in appearance.

A color photograph accompanies each pattern, along with a list of the techniques used and reference pages for directions. Read over the techniques and suggestions before beginning your appliqué. The following patterns finish to a 16" x 16" square. Remember to cut your background fabric 2" larger than the finished size of the block, squaring up the blocks to the cut size when completed.

Patterns for these blocks appear on the pullout patterns.

Pattern 1: Pansies and Primroses

Block size: 16" x 16"

The simple elegance of pansies and primroses combines with the delicate curves of vines and leaves in this arrangement. Perfect for any skill level, this pattern gives you an opportunity to try stippling. Remember the pansies are the focus, so choose primrose fabrics to complement them.

Refer to the pullout insert pages at the back of the book for the full-size pattern. For turned leaves, refer to page 30. To preconstruct petals, see "Preconstruction" on page 28. Use the cut-to-shape technique on pages 25–26 for the stems.

1. Prepare the background block as described on pages 17–18.
2. Preconstruct the turned and split leaves, 1/2, 3/4, 5/6, 7/8/9, 10/11, and 12/13. Be sure to use a strong value change in the two fabrics you choose for these leaves.
3. Appliqué stems 14 and 15 behind the primroses to the left of the pansies. Appliquéing the stems in two segments instead of one continuous segment prevents the stem fabric from creating shadows under light-value flowers.
4. Appliqué pansy outer and inner petals 16–23.
5. Appliqué pansy outer and inner petals 24–30 and pansy center 31.
6. Preconstruct the star-shaped elements 35, 38, and 41 onto pansy petals 34, 37, and 40 as shown. Appliqué pansy outer and inner petals 32–33, 34/35/36, 37/38/39, 40/41 and center 42.
7. For each primrose, select a range of related colors for the petals to provide the best effect. Appliqué the primroses, using pieces 43–84. Leave the side of petal 74 free where it overlaps petal 82. After you appliqué petal 82, finish appliquéing petal 74. Use either direct or reverse appliqué for the primrose centers, 57, 68, 73, and 84.
8. Appliqué pansy petals 85–90 and center 91.
9. Appliqué small turned-leaf 92/94.
10. Appliqué small leaves 93 and 95–106.
11. Embroider the petal lines on the pansies, or draw them, using permanent ink.

Pattern 2: Lotus Blossom and Grapes

Block size: 16" x 16"

Oriental in feeling, the lotus blossom and grape pattern is a study in natural lines. A variety of color and value is essential in this pattern. To enhance the Oriental feeling, pair a dark background with a pastel lotus blossom.

Refer to the pullout insert pages at the back of the book for the full-size pattern. For turned leaves, refer to page 30. For stems and branches, use the cut-to-shape technique on pages 25–26 . For the grapes, refer to ovals on pages 27–28. For preconstruction of flowers, see page 29.

1. Prepare the background block as described on pages 17–18.
2. Appliqué branches 1 and 2 and stem 3. If your background fabric is suitable, consider using reverse appliqué.
3. Appliqué the lotus bud, 4, 5, and 6. Appliqué the gladiolus bud, 7–13, and gladiolus leaves 14 and 15.
4. Appliqué water lily leaf back 16.
5. Appliqué leaves 17–19.
6. Appliqué water lily leaf back 20, then leaf top 21.
7. Appliqué stem 22, then leaves 23–28.

8. Appliqué grapes 29–45, lotus petal 46, then grape 47. For the overlapping grapes, try working in a gradation of value or a variety of colors so the grapes won't look like a lump of fabric.
9. Appliqué stem 48, then leaves 49–53.
10. Appliqué tiny leaf 54, then small flowers 55 and 56. Appliqué leaves 57–60.
11. Appliqué grapes 61–74, then turned lotus petal 75/76. Appliqué tiny leaves 77 and 78.
12. Appliqué tiny leaves and flowers 79–82, then flower petals/flowers 83–88. Appliqué tiny leaf 89, then flowers 90 and 91. If you wish, preconstruct these small flowers and tiny leaves, then appliqué the unit in place to the right of the lotus blossom. Preconstruct the flower centers with reverse appliqué, embellish with embroidery, or draw them later.
13. Appliqué lotus petals 92–114. Petal combinations 100/101 and 110/111 are turned petals, showing undersides. Piece 112 can be used as the lotus "center" by placing darker colors there.

Pattern 3: Maple Leaves, Gourds, and Anemones

Block size: 16" x 16"

I drew the gourds using yellow summer squash as models. Keep this in mind when selecting fabric, for a specific seasonal feel. Yellow adds a touch of summer. If you choose fabric to make them look like gourds, combining them with maple leaves brings to mind the spectacular fall palette. The hibiscus and anemones provide a reminder of warmer weather.

Refer to the pullout insert pages at the back of the book for the full-size pattern. Try the liquid-glue technique described on page 28 for the star-shaped gourd ends and anemone centers. For the cut-to-shape technique, refer to pages 25–26. Stippling vein lines and edges on the maple leaves adds an extra dimensional touch; instructions for stippling appear on pages 30–31.

1. Prepare the background block as described on pages 17–18.
2. Appliqué gourd 1 and star-shaped end 2.
3. Appliqué maple leaf 3. If the points on the maple leaves are difficult, round the points slightly.
4. Appliqué second gourd 4 and star-shaped end 5.
5. Appliqué maple leaves 6–12.
6. Appliqué tiny leaf 13, then anemone petals 14 and 15. Appliqué tiny leaf 16, then appliqué petals 17 and 18, and flower center 19.
7. Appliqué tiny leaves 20 and 21, then anemone petals 22–25, and center 26.
8. Appliqué tiny leaves 27 and 28, then petals 29–34 and flower center 35. Appliqué tiny leaf 36. Appliqué flower petals 37–38, tiny leaf 39, and petals 40–41, 43–44, and flower centers 42 and 45.
9. For branches 46–48, use the cut-to-shape technique. Leave a small section of 46 free where 47 lies under it. After appliquéing 47, finish the open section on 46.
10. Appliqué anemone petals 49–52, center 53, and tiny leaves 54–57. Appliqué anemone petals 58–61, 63–66, and centers 62 and 67. Appliqué tiny leaves 68 and 69, anemone petals 70–73, then center 74.
11. Appliqué hibiscus petals 75–79, then flower centers 80 and 81.

Pattern 4: Iris and Fuchsias

Block size: 16" x 16"

If you choose an assortment of fabrics from the wide range of hand-dyed and batik fabrics available, the iris will look as if it were cut fresh from the garden. Be sure to use a full palette of greens for the leaves, adding different values as well.

Refer to the pullout insert pages at the back of the book for the full-size pattern. For turned leaves and petals, refer to page 30. For stems, use the cut-to-shape technique on pages 25–26.

1. Prepare the background block as described on pages 17–18.
2. Appliqué stem 1, then leaves 2–14.
3. Appliqué turned leaves 15/16, 17/18, 19/20, iris calyx 21, and iris stalk 22.
4. Appliqué iris leaf 23 (a continuation of turned leaf 19/20), then buds 24–28, and stalks 29–30.
5. Appliqué leaves 31–35, then fuchsia stems 36–38.
6. Appliqué turned camellia leaf 39/40, petals 41 and 42, then turned petals 43/44, 45/46/47, and 48/49. Appliqué petal 50.
7. Appliqué camellia center 51 and appliqué or embroider center details 52–57.
8. Appliqué fuchsia petals 58–63, 64–68, and 69–73. Leave the upper tip of petal 71 free until you have appliquéd 72, then finish 71.
9. Appliqué iris petal undersides 74 and 75, turned petal 76/77, "beard" 78, petals 79 and 80, beard 81, petals 82–84, and beard 85.
10. Embroider fuchsia stamens 86–91.

Pattern 5: Tulips and Poinsettia

Block size: 16" x 16"

Although anemones appear in abundance on this pattern, the focus flowers are the tulips and the poinsettia. From fiery red to pale green and white, poinsettias will work on any background fabric. Be sure to change values in tulip petals 107–11 to show the inside of the petals. Sprinkle berries among the anemones for added sparkle. The berries in "Barbara's Bloomin' Birthday" on page 42 were made using the index-card technique as shown on page 27.

Refer to the pullout insert pages at the back of the book for the full-size pattern. Try the cut-to-shape technique on pages 25–26 for the tulip stems. For the anemone and poinsettia centers, try the liquid glue technique given on page 28. For turned leaves and petals, refer to page 30.

1. Prepare the background block as described on pages 17–18.
2. Appliqué large leaf 1 (behind the tulip stem and poinsettia). Appliqué tulip stem 2, and turned leaves 3/4 and 5/6. Appliqué tulip stem 7 and turned leaf 8/9.

3. Appliqué leaves 10–18.
4. Appliqué anemone petals and centers, beginning with petal 19 and ending with center 87. Appliqué turned leaf 31/32 after appliquéing center 30. Be sure to appliqué petal 38 on the poinsettia before completing the rest of the anemones. Appliqué leaves 57 and 63 in their numerical sequence.
5. Appliqué poinsettia petals 88–96 and turned petal 97/98. Appliqué petal 99, then center 100.
6. Appliqué tulip petals 101–4, 105, and 106. Appliqué turned petals 107/110 and 108/109, then petal 111.
7. Appliqué anemone petals and centers 112–29.

❧Note❧

The Tulips and Poinsettia block shown in the photo above was cut 14½" x 14½". A 1"-wide sashing strip was added to each side of the block to make a 16" x 16" finished block.

Pattern 6: Petunias and Sweet Peas

Block size: 16" x 16"

Petunias, zinnias, and sweet peas combine with peperomia and cabbage leaves for a summer arrangement. The flowers 26–28 and 37–39 are unopened blossoms facing left and right.

Refer to the pullout insert pages at the back of the book for the full-size pattern. For the sweet pea stems, use the cut-to-shape technique on pages 25–26 or the reverse-appliqué method on page 24. If you reverse-appliqué these stems, use a single drawn line to create the channel as shown in the Tip on page 24. Or, if you prefer, embroider them. For turned leaves and petals, refer to page 30. For preconstruction of flowers, see page 29.

1. Prepare the background block as described on pages 17–18.
2. Appliqué or embroider stems 1 and 2. Appliqué leaf 3 (behind the zinnia stem), then appliqué stems 4 and 5.
3. Preconstruct peperomia leaves 6/7, 8/9, 10/11, 12/13, and 14/15, then appliqué them to the block. Try both direct and reverse appliqué when preconstructing any flower.

4. Appliqué petunia petals 16–22, then appliqué center 23 and 24 (or embroider center 24).
5. Appliqué leaf 25 and flower bud petals 26–28.
6. Appliqué petals 29–32 and center 33.
7. Appliqué ornamental cabbage leaves 34–36 and flower bud petals 37/38/39. Draw with permanent ink or embroider the vein lines on the cabbage leaves.
8. Appliqué petals 40–45 and flower center 46.
9. Appliqué petunia petals 47–50, center 51, and petals 52 and 53, centers 54 and 55 (or embroider center 55), then petals 56 and 57. Embroider flower center details on center 51.
10. Appliqué sweet pea petals 58–67 and 68–85.
11. Appliqué zinnia petals and center 86–96 and 97–113.

Pattern 7: Daffodils and Mums

Block size: 16" x 16"

Daffodils, chrysanthemums, apples, and baby pumpkins, delightfully combined, make a lovely cross-seasonal arrangement. Cut the baby pumpkins in the foreground from a single piece of fabric, or appliqué from several fabrics for more dimension. Remember to use several value changes for the leaves under the daffodils and the grapes for clear delineation of each piece. Refer to the pullout insert pages at the back of the book for the full-size pattern. For turned leaves, refer to page 30. For stems and grass, use the cut-to-shape technique on pages 25–26. For grapes, refer to ovals on pages 27–28 and see pages 30–31 for stippling directions.

1. Prepare the background block as described on pages 17–18.
2. Appliqué apples 1/2 and 3/4/5. Apple 1/2 is inverted, with its blossom side on top, and apple 3/4/5 is "right side up."
3. Strips 6–12 are strips of cut palm leaf. Cut each strip on the bias to prevent puckering. Appliqué in place.
4. Appliqué lower leaves 13–16 and turned leaves 17/18 and 19/20.
5. Appliqué grapes 21–34.
6. Appliqué daffodil petals 35–44 and center 45, then daffodil petals 46–55 and center 56.
7. Appliqué left pumpkin (sections 57–62), then right pumpkin (sections 63–72). Appliqué center 73 and stem 74.
8. Appliqué grapes 75 and 76.
9. Appliqué turned leaf 77/78 and leaf 79.
10. Appliqué stems 80 and 81, then leaves 82, 83, turned leaf 84/85, and leaf 86.
11. Appliqué chrysanthemum petals 87–107, center 108, petals 109–26, and center 127. Remember to cut from behind each petal to eliminate bulk.
12. If desired, stipple leaf 79 to create shading, referring to the illustration below.

Leaf 79

Pattern 8: Peony and Orchid

Block size: 16" x 16"

An orchid, a tulip, and a peony, plus tiny flowers, berries, and buds on stalks provide a variety of shapes and textures. The little "innys" of the peony petals give this flower its natural quality. Be patient—it's worth it! Refer to the pullout insert pages at the back of the book for the full-size pattern. To preconstruct turned leaves and flowers, see "Preconstruction" on pages 28-30. For index-card berries, see page 27. For the peony ruffles, use the liquid-glue technique on page 28.

1. Prepare the background block as described on pages 17–18.
2. Appliqué branch 1. This branch is perfect for reverse appliqué.
3. Preconstruct veins 3 and 4 on leaf 2, then appliqué leaf 2 to the block. Appliqué turned leaf 5/6.
4. Appliqué stems 7–9.
5. Appliqué double leaf 10 at the end of stem 9.
6. Appliqué tulip petals 11–16.
7. Appliqué tiny leaves 17–22, tiny stem 23, and stem 24. Appliqué leaf 25 and buds 26–29.

8. Appliqué stem 30, then petals 31 and 32, and center 33. Appliqué petals 34–38 and center 39; use a darker value for centers 33 and 39 to give the appearance of looking inside the blossom.
9. Appliqué peony leaves 40–45. Appliqué peony petals 46–64. (Consider preconstructing petal 51/52.) Appliqué peony stamens 65; consider cutting this piece from black or other dark-colored fabric to give the appearance of looking down into the flower.
10. Appliqué peony petals 66–70.
11. Appliqué orchid petals 71–81. Appliqué orchid bud petals 82–84, 85, and 86. If you can find the perfect fabric for the orchid center, eliminate petals 77–79.
12. Appliqué tiny leaves 87–90 and berries 91–94. Appliqué tiny leaves 95–101 and berries 102–6. Appliqué tiny leaf 107 and berries 108–12.
13. Appliqué tiny leaves 113–16 and berries 117–21.

Pattern 9: Roses and Daisies

Block size: 16" x 16"

For the lover of intricate appliqué, this block offers wonderful possibilities. The pyracantha and vine accent the simple shapes of the leaves, offsetting the intricacy of the roses and daisies. For me, roses are possibly the most challenging flower to translate into fabric. Try achieving the illusion of depth by stippling, following the illustrations on pages 30-31. If you use the cut-to-shape technique for the pyracantha branch, cut it on the bias to prevent puckering. Cut and appliqué this stem in one piece, allowing spaces between the berries to show through. Refer to the pullout insert pages at the back of the book for the full-size pattern. Needle-turn the berries as shown on pages 19–20. To preconstruct leaves or petals, see pages 28–29. For stems, use cut-to-shape appliqué as shown on pages 25–26.

1. Prepare the background block as described on pages 17–18.
2. Appliqué pyracantha stem 1.
3. Preconstruct vein lines in background leaves 2/3, 4/5, and 6/7. Appliqué them in place.
4. Appliqué stem 8.
5. Preconstruct vein lines in background leaves 9/10, 11/12, 13/14, 15/16, 17/18, 19/20, and 21/22. Appliqué them in place.
6. Appliqué tiny pyracantha leaves 23–25, then berries 26–28. I needle-turned these berries for a more natural appearance, using dark blue fabrics for some to suggest unripened berries.
7. Appliqué tiny pyracantha leaves 34 and 35, berries 29–46, leaves 47 and 48, then berries 49–77.
8. Appliqué daisy petals 78–101, then center 102. Appliqué daisy petals 103–118, then center 119.
9. For the upper rose, appliqué petals 120–43.
10. Appliqué leaves 144–61.

✥*Note*✥

Do not appliqué leaves 207–9 until the rose below them is appliquéd.

11. Appliqué center rose's petals 162–78, then lower rose petals 179–206.
12. Appliqué leaves 207–9.

Pattern 10: Camellias and Lilacs

Block size: 16" x 16"

The classic marriage of camellias and lilacs comes straight from my grandmother's garden. She had an amazing green thumb. I can appliqué all those beauties even if I can't grow them! The bract 103–148 works well in bright colors—reds, pinks, oranges, and yellows.

Refer to the pullout insert pages at the back of the book for the full-size pattern. To preconstruct vein lines, see pages 28-29. For tulip stamens 30 and stems, use the cut-to-shape technique on pages 25-26. For the liquid-glue technique, refer to page 28.

1. Prepare the background block as described on pages 17–18.
2. Appliqué background leaf 1, stems 2 and 3, then leaves 4–7.
3. Appliqué stem 8, then preconstruct the vein lines on cut palm leaf 9/10. Appliqué turned leaf 11.
4. Appliqué unopened camellia petals 12–18.
5. Appliqué background leaf 19.
6. Appliqué stem 20 using the cut-to-shape technique or reverse appliqué. Make the stem wider if you feel uncomfortable with the narrow width, or embroider the stem using several rows of embroidery.
7. Appliqué the tulip petals on the left. Preconstruct petals 21/22, 23/24, 25/26/27, and 28/29; appliqué in place. Appliqué center 30, then preconstruct and appliqué petals 31/32.
8. Appliqué camellia leaf 33.
9. Appliqué the lilacs, 34–90. Don't get lost in the lilacs! These pieces should give the impression of blossoms. Just appliqué one shape after another, one by one, until your lilacs come into bloom.
10. Appliqué tulip petal 91, then stem 92.
11. Appliqué leaves 93–102 along stem 92.
12. Appliqué bracts 103–48 along stem 20. None of the petals lie under the stem. Petals may overlap the stem and/or other petals.
13. Appliqué camellia petals 149–55. Preconstruct petals 156/157 and 158/159, then appliqué each completed petal in place. Appliqué petals 160 and 161, then preconstruct petal 162/163 and appliqué in place.
14. Appliqué camellia center 164. Try painting the seam allowances of the camellia centers with liquid fabric glue.
15. Appliqué camellia leaf 165, then camellia petals 166–75. Preconstruct petal 176/177, then appliqué in place. Appliqué petal 178, then flower center 179, following the directions for appliquéing center 164 in step 14.

Pattern 11: Anemones and Anthurium

Block size: 16" x 16"

Color…color…color…anemones in a rainbow of colors add just the right touch to this pattern. Work to keep the curves smooth on all the leaf shapes to give the appearance of lacy edges around the perimeter of the design.

Refer to the pullout insert pages at the back of the book for the full-size pattern. For reverse-appliquéd stems, see page 24. For grass leaves, use the cut-to-shape technique on pages 25–26. For preconstruction of flower centers 121–31, see page 29.

1. Prepare the background block as described on pages 17–18.
2. Appliqué stems 1, 2, and 3.
3. Appliqué oak leaf 4, noting where it lies under several of the small flowers.
4. Appliqué stem 5, using reverse appliqué if desired.
5. Appliqué large leaf 6, then tiny leaves 7–22.
6. Appliqué large leaves 23 and 24, then small flower petals 25–29. Appliqué center 30, then large leaves 31 and 32. Continue appliquéing small flower petals and centers in numerical order, ending with petal 55 and center 56.
7. Appliqué grass leaves 57–59, then anthurium 60–61. (This anthurium center may be preconstructed.)
8. Appliqué small flower petals 62–71 and centers 67 and 72.
9. Appliqué lower stem 73, using reverse appliqué if desired. Appliqué tiny leaves 74–83.
10. Appliqué leaves 84–90, then primrose petals 91–95 and 97–102. Appliqué centers 96 and 103.
11. Appliqué large center oak leaf 104.
12. Appliqué stems 105 and 106.
13. Preconstruct the centers of flowers 107–17 using reverse appliqué, then appliqué flowers in place.
14. Appliqué tiny stems 118–20. Preconstruct flower centers 121–31 as directed in step 13, then appliqué in place.
15. Appliqué flower petals 132–41, then petals 142–49.
16. Embroider stamens on petals 137, 139, and 144.

Pattern 12: Roses and Pears

Block size: 16" x 16"

Roses combined with baby bosc pears, anthurium, freesias, and camellias give the full range of nature's bounty in this pattern. Don't forget the pears can be ripened or unripened. Add a touch of color to the pears by brushing them with powdered blush-on!

Refer to the pullout insert pages at the back of the book for the full-size pattern. For stems, use the cut-to-shape technique on pages 25–26. For preconstruction, see pages 28–30. For shading the roses, see "Stippling" on pages 30–31.

1. Prepare the background block as described on pages 17–18.

2. Appliqué leaf 1 at left and stem segments 2, 3, and 4.

3. Appliqué leaves 5–10 and stems 11–14 across the top of the block.

4. Appliqué bosc pear 15, then stem segments 16 and 17. Appliqué leaf 18, pear 19, centers 20 and 21, and leaves 22–24. Appliqué tiny piece 25 where stems 13 and 14 meet. Appliqué leaves 26–29, pears 30, 32 and 33, and pear center 31.

5. Appliqué rose leaves 34 and 35 and rose petal 36.

6. Appliqué anthurium 37, 39, and 41, and centers 38, 40, and 42. These centers may be preconstructed with direct or reverse appliqué.

7. Appliqué rose leaf 43, then rose petals 44–59. Appliqué rosebud stem 60, then rose petals 61–73.

8. Appliqué freesia petals 74–76, then freesia stem 77. Appliqué freesia petals 78–89.

9. Appliqué rosebud petals 90–98, 99–101, calyx 102.

10. Appliqué lower flower petals 103–8 and center 109.

11. Appliqué petals 110–16, 118–25, and 127–33. Appliqué flower centers 117 and 126.

COMPLEMENTARY BLOCKS

Use the complementary blocks with the feature blocks or as separate blocks for other projects. Each block features an individual flower, fruit, or vine. On the 8" x 8" blocks, the design continues into the seam allowance. Remember to add appropriate seam allowances when cutting out the appliqué pieces.

Start by making a master pattern before you appliqué. Refer to the instructions given in the "Pattern Making" section of "Preparing the Block" on pages 17–18. Patterns for the blocks are on pages 84–96.

Oak Leaf

Block size: 8" x 8"

Try a separate color or value for each oak leaf to enhance the visual effect. For a creative option, appliqué berries "sprinkled" randomly over the block.

These leaves benefit noticeably from stippling. Begin by stippling around the outside edges and then shade in the center of the leaves.

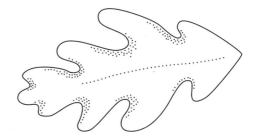

1. Prepare the background block as described on pages 17–18.
2. Appliqué the oak leaves in numerical order, clipping inside curves as necessary.

Camellias

Morning Glories

Block size: 8" x 8"

Vary the value of the camellia petals for dimensional illusion. Be sure to extend the leaf pieces along the edge of the block a full ¼" into the seam allowance so they can be included securely into the seam when sewing the blocks together. Since the flowers overlap, include an obvious value change between the blossoms. Remember to cut away the background fabric after each petal is appliquéd.

1. Prepare the background block as described on pages 17–18.
2. Appliqué leaves 1–3, leaves 4–8, petals 9 and 10, and leaf 11.
3. Appliqué petals 12–17, center 18, and petals 19–21.
4. Appliqué turned petal 22/23, petal 24, and turned petal 25/26. Appliqué center 27.

Block size: 8" x 8"

Before appliquéing each blossom, draw the center and vein lines, using dye pens, Pigma™ pens, or embroidery. Whichever technique you choose to do, extend the lines a full ¼" into the seam allowance so none of the edges will show after being appliquéd. For the stems, use the cut-to-shape technique on pages 25–26. For turned leaves, see page 30.

1. Prepare the background block as described on pages 17–18.
2. Appliqué stem 1 and leaves 2–7. Appliqué stem 8, leaf 9, and stem 10.
3. Appliqué leaf 11, stem 12, and leaf 13. Appliqué stem 14.
4. Appliqué flowers 15 and 16, leaf 17, turned leaf 18/19, and leaf 20.
5. Appliqué flower 21, bud petals 22 and 23, and calyx pieces 24 and 25.
6. Appliqué stem 26, turned leaf 27/28, and stem 29.
7. Appliqué flower 30.

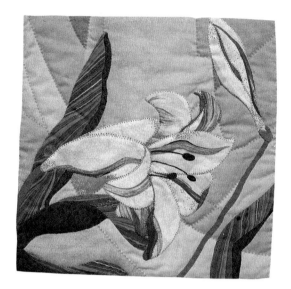

Grape Cluster

Lily

Block size: 8" x 8"

To keep the grape clusters from looking like lumps of the same fabric, vary the values or colors of the grapes. Be sure to extend pieces along the edge of the block a full ¼" into the seam allowance so they can be included securely into the seam when sewing the blocks together. For stems, use the cut-to-shape technique on pages 25–26. For ovals, see pages 27–28.

1. Prepare the background block as described on pages 17–18.
2. Appliqué stems 1, 2, and 3. Use the cut-to-shape technique. Appliqué leaves 4–11.
3. Appliqué grapes 12–16 in the lower corner, and grapes 17–43 in the large cluster.
4. Embroider or draw the curled vines, 44–46.

Block size: 8" x 8"

For fun, try working with stripes for the lily. (See "La Petite Fleur" on page 43.) For stems, see pages 25–26 for the cut-to-shape technique. For turned leaves, refer to page 30.

1. Prepare the background block as described on pages 17–18.
2. Place bud petal 1 in position and baste in place with unknotted thread. Do not appliqué.
3. Appliqué stem 2. Cut the stem on the bias to prevent puckering.
4. Appliqué bud petals 3 and 4 over petal 1 and remove basting from bud 1.
5. Appliqué turned leaves 5/6, 7/8, 9/10, and 11/12.
6. Appliqué lily stem 13, petal 14, and turned petals 15/16, 17/18, 19/20, and 21/22. Appliqué petal 23 and turned petal 24/25.
7. Draw or embroider the stamens.

Carolina Jessamine

Sunflower

Block size: 8" x 8"

Extend each leaf or petal piece at the edge of the block a full ¼" into the seam allowance so it can be included securely into the seam when sewing the blocks together. For stems, see the reverse-appliqué technique on page 24 or the cut-to-shape technique on pages 25–26.

1. Prepare the background block as described on pages 17–18.
2. Appliqué flower petals 1 and 2 in the lower right corner.
3. Appliqué stem 3, using the cut-to-shape technique. Appliqué leaves 4–6, 7–9, and petals 10 and 11.
4. Reverse-appliqué stem 12, then appliqué leaves 13–17.
5. Appliqué stem 18 using the cut-to-shape technique, then appliqué leaves 19–27. Appliqué flower buds 28, 29, and 30–32; flower petals 33–39 and 41–45; and centers 40 and 46.

Block size: 8" x 8"

Although the sunflower has many pieces, each piece's shape is not difficult, so the appliqué goes quickly. Trim background fabric away from as many of the sunflower petals as safely possible to reduce bulk in the block. For stems, refer to the cut-to-shape technique on pages 25–26. For turned leaves, see page 30.

1. Prepare the background block as described on pages 17–18.
2. Appliqué stems 1–5. Appliqué leaves 6–9.
3. Appliqué sunflower petals 10–46 and center 47.
4. Appliqué turned leaf 48/49, bud petals 50–52, leaf 53, bud petal 54, and turned leaf 55/56.

VINE BLOCKS

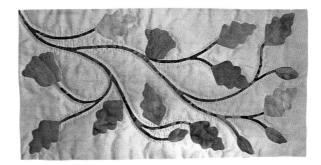

Vine with Leaves and Berries

Vine with Buds and Blossoms

Block size: 8" x 16"

The gentle S-curves on these vines represent my favorite shape to appliqué. Work to keep the lines flowing, free from bumps and angles. Peggy Cord used a large-scale floral print in sections of her vine, creating an interesting play of value. (See the photo on page 42.) "In Bloom" on page 36 features vines of many different greens.

1. Prepare the background block as described on pages 17–18.
2. Appliqué stem 1, using either the cutwork technique on page 25 or reverse appliqué on page 24.
3. With a chalk marker, lightly mark lines to indicate the finished block size before appliquéing the leaves. These lines provide a guide for leaf placement, ensuring that they won't extend into the seam allowance.
4. Appliqué leaves 2–13, using a variety of leaf fabrics for greater visual interest.
5. Appliqué berries 14–21. Just when you thought it was safe—more index-card berries! The berry color can be the added punch that "makes" the entire block.

Block size: 8" x 16"

For a change of season, these vines have the addition of blossoms and buds. Susan B. Elliott used a medium-scale overall print for the vines in her quilt "In Hope of Entwives." Remember to view your fabric selection in ¼"-wide sections to see if it is suitable for vines.

1. Prepare the background block as described on pages 17–18.
2. Appliqué stem 1, using either the cutwork technique on page 25 or reverse appliqué on page 24.
3. With a chalk marker lightly mark lines to indicate the finished block size before appliquéing the leaves. These lines provide a guide for leaf placement, ensuring that they won't extend into the seam allowance.
4. Appliqué leaves 2–10, using a variety of leaf fabrics for greater visual interest.
5. Appliqué flower petals 11–21 and buds 22–25, 26–29, 30–33, and 34–37. Use a variety of colors and values.

CORNERSTONES

The idea for these small blocks came from Dee Shaffer of Texarkana, Texas. While constructing her quilt "Garden View" on page 39, Dee chose a more traditional setting that required sashings and cornerstones. She originally chose to appliqué a single oak leaf in each square, using a leaf pattern from the oak leaf border/complementary block. This single leaf looked too simple, however, compared to the complexity of the feature blocks. Dee solved this problem by choosing one blossom from one of the feature blocks to combine with each oak leaf, providing a spectacular effect, as you can see. Many thanks to Dee for sharing her idea. Choose one or more of the following blocks, or play with this idea to produce exciting results of your own.

As you design your own quilt sets, keep these smaller blocks in mind when choosing combinations of blocks and separator strips. Use as many of the components as you like. Each provides its own special quality—used together, they enhance the entire design of the quilt. Patterns for the blocks are on pages 84–96.

Refer to the section on pages 33–34 for "Sashing with Cornerstones" when setting these cornerstone blocks into your quilt.

Pattern 1: Oak Leaf with Daisy

Block size: 4" x 4"
1. Prepare the background block as described on pages 17–18.
2. Appliqué oak leaf 1.
3. Appliqué daisy petals 2–17.
4. Appliqué center 18.

Pattern 2: Oak Leaf with Two Anemones

Block size: 4" x 4"
1. Prepare the background block as described on pages 17–18.
2. Appliqué oak leaf 1.
3. Appliqué petals 2–5 and center 6.
4. Appliqué petals 7–11 and center 12.

Pattern 3: Oak Leaf with Fuchsia I

Block size: 4" x 4"

1. Prepare the background block as described on pages 17–18.
2. Appliqué oak leaf 1.
3. Appliqué stem 2.
4. Appliqué petals 3–5, leaving the tip of petal 5 open where it crosses petal 6.
5. Appliqué petal 6, then complete the appliqué for petal 5. Appliqué petal 7.
6. Draw, using permanent ink, or embroider the stamens.

Pattern 5: Oak Leaf with Fuchsia II

Block size: 4" x 4"

1. Prepare the background block as described on pages 17–18.
2. Appliqué oak leaf 1.
3. Appliqué fuchsia petals 2–7.

Pattern 4: Oak Leaf with Primrose

Block size: 4" x 4"

1. Prepare the background block as described on pages 17–18.
2. Appliqué oak leaf 1.
3. Appliqué petals 2–11.
4. Appliqué center 12.

Pattern 6: Oak Leaf with Three Anemones

Block size: 4" x 4"

1. Prepare the background block as described on pages 17–18.
2. Appliqué oak leaf 1.
3. Appliqué flower petals 2–7, 9–13, and 15–19.
4. Appliqué centers 8, 14, and 20.

SPACERS

Several of the quilts pictured in the Gallery feature dogtooth borders used as sashing. When made in short strips, they become spacer strips. When groups of blocks are set together in an asymmetrical quilt set, spacers are added in areas to fit the blocks together evenly. I chose dogtooth triangles for spacers because of their timeless connection to appliqué. Look for other designs that could be used in this manner.

Any of the spacers in this section make very attractive borders. The only adjustment you must make to the following instructions is to increase the length of the spacer to match the length of the quilt. Use these borders in combination with other pieced, appliquéd, or plain borders for any appliqué project.

The instructions on the following pages include the traditional dogtooth construction, plus two updated versions: the gradated dogtooth and the zigzag variation.

Traditional Dogtooth Spacer

Traditionally, dogtooth borders are done in two colors. For quilts made using the blocks in this book, try using the spacers as a place for additional fabrics that add sparkle to the quilt.

For the spacers, begin by determining the length of the finished strip. This measurement determines the length of the base of the dogtooth triangle.

Dogtooth triangles are more similar to equilateral triangles than to the right-angle triangles in sawtooth or half-square triangle designs.

Equilateral triangle

Right-angle triangle

For dogtooth borders, the length of the base of each triangle is the same as the height of the triangle, so the length of the triangle base also determines the width of the spacer strips.

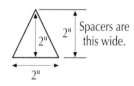

Spacers are this wide.

The spacer must always be divided equally so that the triangles fill the space evenly. The illustration shows a 12"-long spacer strip with "teeth" (triangles) each measuring 2" at the base. This 2" length requires the triangle's height to be 2", so that the width of the spacer will be 2", finished.

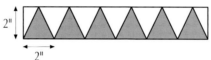

If a 12"-long spacer has teeth 3" wide at the base, the spacer will be 3" wide, finished.

Designing a Dogtooth Border

These triangles are not true equilateral triangles since all three sides are not equal. If the height of the triangle (the line drawn from the midpoint of the base to the apex) is the same as the length of the base, the base will be slightly shorter than the two sides of the triangle. For example, if the base's length is 2" and the triangle's height is 2", the length of the sides will be 2¼".

To figure the size of the triangle and placement along the spacer strip, draw a line on graph paper, measuring the length of the triangle's base.

At the midpoint of this line (1"), draw a perpendicular line of the same length (2").

Draw a line on each side, connecting the triangle base line and the perpendicular line as shown. This is the triangle needed for your spacer.

Remember to consider the scale of the triangles when designing these spacers. A dogtooth triangle too large for the other design elements might overpower the entire project. Experiment on paper with your block set to determine the correct size for your quilt.

1. Determine the size needed for the equilateral triangle "tooth," then make a plastic template following these measurements, adding a ¼"-wide seam allowance only to the base of the triangle.

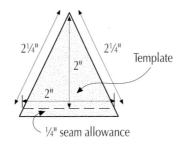

Add ¼" seam allowance only to base of template.

For the template neither side requires the addition of a seam allowance.

2. Prepare your design and background fabrics by cutting a strip of each fabric measuring 2" wider and 2" longer than the finished size. These strips will be squared up when the appliqué is complete.

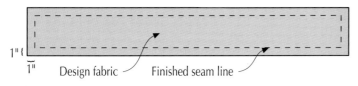

3. Starting at least 1" away from the left edge of your design fabric, trace the first triangle by aligning the base of the triangle with the bottom edge of the fabric. After tracing this first triangle, place a small dot on the background ¼" above the point of the triangle. Move 2" to the side of this center dot and place another dot as shown.

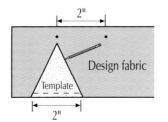

Trace triangle onto design fabric; align with dots.

4. Align the center point of the template with this dot and draw the next tooth.

5. Continue drawing points, placing templates, and drawing triangles, until you have drawn all the triangles necessary for the spacer. The length of the triangle's base matches the distance between the dots; for example, 2" triangles require a 2" space between the dots; 3" triangles require a 3" space, and so on.

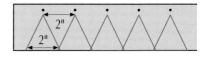

6. Pin the design fabric on top of the background fabric, right sides up. Baste inside the drawn lines and begin to appliqué, turning under the seam allowance along the drawn line for cutwork appliqué as shown on page 25.

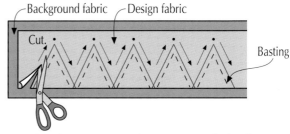

7. Complete the entire strip, then trim away the background fabric from behind the triangles, leaving a ¼"-wide seam allowance. Square up the strip to the required size.

Gradated Dogtooth Spacer

Adding gradated fabrics adds a special quality to the dogtooth spacer. The change in value or color of these fabrics creates movement within the quilt, as the viewer's eye follows these changes. For an example of this technique, see "In Bloom" on page 36.

1. Follow the instructions given for dogtooth spacers on pages 65–66. Instead of drawing the "teeth" all at once on a long strip, trace each triangle individually, one gradation at a time.

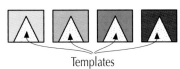

Templates

2. Draw around the template and then cut out each triangle, adding ¼"-wide seam allowances only on the right and left sides of the tooth. (Remember, the ¼"-wide seam allowance has been added to the base of the template.)

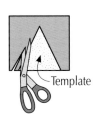

Template

3. Using the triangle template and referring to step 3 on page 66, mark the center dots on the background fabric.

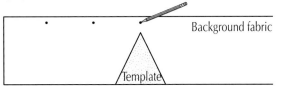

Background fabric

Template

4. Place the fabric triangle on the background strip, aligning the center point of the triangle with the dot on the background fabric and keeping raw edges even along the base. Baste in place, then appliqué the two sides of the triangle to the background block.

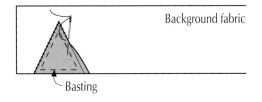

Background fabric

Basting

5. Each time you add a new triangle, align the center of the triangle with the dot. Pin in place, baste, and appliqué.

6. Trim away the background fabric behind the triangles as you finish each one. Square the strip to the required dimensions when completed.

Zigzag Spacer

This spacer gives the illusion of a ribbon twisting behind the blocks.

Direct-Appliqué Zigzag Spacer

1. Follow the instructions given in steps 1–5 on page 66 for the traditional dogtooth spacer. On the design fabric, draw an additional triangle ½" inside the seam line of the first triangle. The second line forms the zigzag.

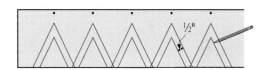

½"

2. Place the design-fabric rectangle on top of the background-fabric rectangle. Baste inside the zigzag and begin your appliqué, cutting a ¼"-wide seam allowance as you work.

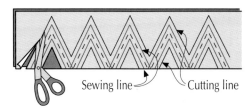

Sewing line   Cutting line

3. Complete the inside line of stitching on all the triangles first, then appliqué the outside line.

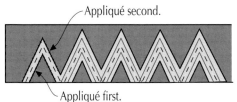

Appliqué second.

Appliqué first.

Reverse-Appliqué Zigzag Spacer

1. Follow the instructions given in steps 1–5 on page 66 for the traditional dogtooth spacer. On the background fabric, draw an additional triangle ½" inside the seam line of the first triangle. The second line forms the zigzag. Refer to the illustration in step 1 for "Direct-Appliqué Zigzag Spacer."

2. Place the design-fabric rectangle under the background-fabric rectangle with right sides up. Baste outside the zigzag and inside the small lower triangles.

3. Following the instructions given on pages 24–25 for reverse appliqué, begin to appliqué, working along the small triangles first, then along the outer edge of the zigzag.

❧ Note ❧

Both zigzag spacers can be done in gradated or two-color zigzag. (See "In Hope of Entwives" on page 43.) Follow steps 1–5 for gradated dogtooth spacers on page 67, adding the ½" seam line required to form the zigzag.

APPLIQUÉ BORDERS

Each of the following two border patterns borrows elements from the feature and complementary blocks. To plan an appliqué border, start by making a full-size drawing of the border from the pullout pattern insert so that any adjustments can be made before sewing. This drawing may be time-consuming, but trying to make things fit later is even more frustrating.

Prepare a piece of paper the length and width of the border. (You may need to tape several pieces of paper together.) Trace the complete pattern onto the paper. Start with the corners and work toward the middle; any adjustments will be made after you finish drawing the pattern.

If the pattern fits perfectly, you have a guardian angel. If it needs adjustment, play with the border until the design suits you. Shorten vines or replace one flower size smaller or larger.

Experiment with borders; make them all the same or choose an asymmetrical border with appliqué on two sides only.

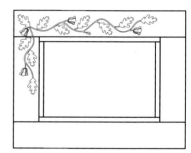

Include an uneven number of borders; for example, add two or three borders on the top and bottom only. This is contemporary floral appliqué—don't be inhibited. Take risks to please yourself.

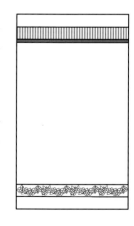

Be sure to cut your border fabric wider and longer by 2" to allow for any shrinkage that may occur while appliquéing. Appliqué the border first, then attach it to the quilt. If you choose to miter the corners on your border, begin appliquéing a few inches away from the mitered corner. If you wish to appliqué over the corners of borders, appliqué the corner section after sewing the borders to the quilt.

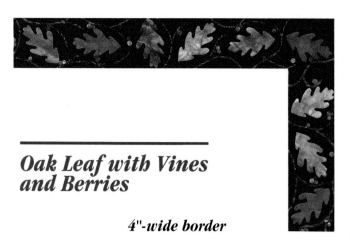

Oak Leaf with Vines and Berries

4"-wide border

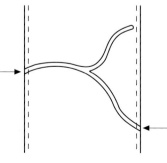

This oak-leaf border was designed to give the impression of falling leaves. Change directions of the leaves more often if you desire. Be sure to allow enough space for the vines to "travel" within the leaves.

1. Measure the quilt top and cut 6½"-wide border strips long enough for your quilt, plus at least 2" for shrinkage during appliqué. (If you are making mitered-corner borders, refer to the directions on page 35 for cutting border strips, remembering to add 3"–4" to the length for appliqué shrinkage.)
2. Following the suggestions given on page 68, construct a paper pattern for your border strips and make adjustments as necessary.
3. Appliqué the leaves, leaving each corner area of the border free until the borders are sewn to the quilt.
4. Appliqué the vines, using either reverse appliqué (page 24) or direct appliqué (page 20). Extend each vine at least ¼" into the seam allowance so that it will be caught securely in the seam on each edge of the border.
5. Prepare and appliqué the berries. Suggested placement of berries is shown, but don't hesitate to scatter the berries across the surface of the border as you wish.
6. Sew borders to the quilt, following the directions on pages 34–35.
7. Appliqué corner sections. Use direct appliqué for stems added at this point.

Anemones with Berries

3"-wide border

This intricate border is spectacular, whether it extends entirely around a quilt or runs along one side, as it does in "La Petite Fleur." (See the photo on page 43.) Select a variety of colors for the anemones. The color photograph shows a sequence of pink, yellow, purple, orange, and blue, repeating throughout the border and causing the viewer's eye to travel along its length. For variety, use different fabrics and values for each flower, and be sure to use several fabrics for the leaves to create visual interest. Refer to the pullout insert pages at the back of the book for the full-size pattern.

Border Section

1. Measure the quilt top and cut 5½"-wide border strips long enough for your quilt, plus at least 2" for shrinkage during appliqué. (If you are making mitered-corner borders, see page 35 for cutting border strips, adding 3"–4" to the length for appliqué shrinkage.)
2. Following the suggestions given on page 68, construct a paper pattern for your border strips and make adjustments as necessary.
3. Starting with leaf 1 in the upper border section, appliqué leaves 1–8 across the top of the border.
4. Appliqué flower petals and centers, beginning with petal 9 in the flower under leaf 1. Appliqué flower petals 10–49 and the flower centers for each anemone.
5. Appliqué the leaves along the side border, starting with leaf 51 at upper left, through leaf 60.
6. Appliqué flower petals and centers, beginning with petal 61 of the flower just next to the corner section. Appliqué flower petals 62–113 and the flower centers for each anemone.
7. If you wish to extend the appliqué along the entire length of each border, repeat the design, adding or subtracting flowers and leaves as needed for a pleasing effect. Stop the appliqué before reaching the corner.
8. Get your index cards ready to use for the berries! Appliqué the berries, paying attention to the difference in the two sizes.
9. If you are appliquéing the border around all 4 sides of the quilt, repeat steps 3–8 for the lower border and second side.

Corner Section

1. Sew appliquéd borders to the quilt top, following the instructions for "Borders with Straight-Cut Corners" on page 34 or "Borders with Mitered Corners" on page 35.

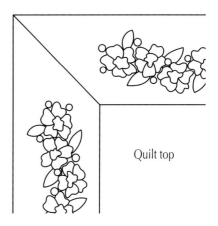

After all four borders are sewn to the quilt top, appliqué each corner section.

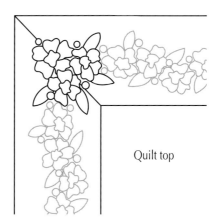

2. Appliqué leaves C1–C4.
3. Appliqué flower petals C5–C21.
4. Appliqué flower centers C10, C16, and C22.
5. Appliqué berries, noting the two sizes.

Quilt Sets

The number and type of blocks you include will determine the way you set your quilt. Try to achieve balance by considering color, value, and block shape. Examine the quilts in the Gallery section for setting ideas. Choose the sets that appeal to you and that include block sizes similar to yours.

The following illustrations show the sets and dimensions of six of the quilts featured in the Gallery. Designing the quilt sets was as exciting for me as creating the blocks.

Suggestions lead to invention—use these plans as illustrated or as ideas for development of your own set.

In Bloom

Finished size: 62" x 82"
Block sizes: 16" x 16", 8" x 8", 8" x 16"
Color photo: page 36

"In Bloom" combines both the 8" x 8" oak leaf blocks and the 8" x 16" vine blocks with the 16" x 16" feature blocks. This quilt set is the signature design for contemporary floral appliqué, because it contains all three sizes of blocks, it includes a variety of background fabrics, and it is asymmetrically set. Follow the block set for this quilt or create your own design using any or all of these patterns.

Fabric Requirements

Background
 Feature blocks .... 1⅝ yds.
 Vine blocks .... 1¼ yds.
 8" x 8" (finished) blocks .... ⅓ yd.
Dogtooth spacers
 Background .... ⅞ yd.
 Design fabric (each of 9 gradations) .... ⅛ yd.
Inner borders* .... ⅝ yd.
Dogtooth borders*
 Background .... 1⅜ yds.
 Design fabric (each of 9 gradations) .... ⅛ yd.
Appliquéd borders* .... 1½ yds.
Outer border .... ⅜ yd.
Assorted fabrics for appliqué
Batting .... 72" x 90"
Backing .... 5 yds.
Binding .... 1 yd.

* Borders cut crosswise from selvage to selvage

Cutting

The dimensions given for the following blocks, spacers, and borders are for cut size, before appliqué. The additional 2" to the cut size allows for shrinkage during appliqué.

 6 feature blocks, each 18½" x 18½"
 7 complementary rectangles, each 10½" x 18½"
 2 complementary blocks, each 10½" x 10½"
 1 dogtooth spacer, 4½" x 12½"
 3 dogtooth spacers, each 4½" x 20½"
 3 dogtooth spacers, each 4½" x 28½"
 8 inner border strips, each 2½" x 42"
 2 dogtooth borders, each 4½" x 72", for sides
 2 dogtooth borders, each 4½" x 52", for top and bottom
 2 Oak Leaf with Vines and Berries borders, each 6½" x 80", for sides
 2 Oak Leaf with Vines and Berries borders, each 6½" x 60", for top and bottom
 8 outer border strips, each 1½" x 44"
 10 strips, each 3" x 42", folded in half lengthwise for French binding (See page 82.)

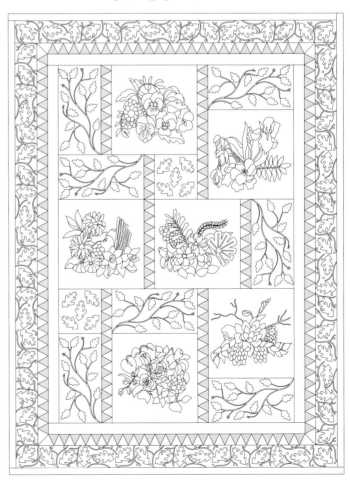

Assembling the Sections

Section 1

1. Prepare, appliqué, and trim 2 feature blocks, 3 vine blocks, and 1 dogtooth spacer, measuring 2½" x 8½", 1 dogtooth spacer measuring 2½" x 16½", and 1 dogtooth spacer measuring 2½" x 24½". (See the instructions given for traditional or gradated dogtooth spacers on pages 65–67.)

2. Sew a 2½" x 16½" dogtooth spacer to an 8½" x 16½" vine block, then sew a 16½" x 16½" feature block to this unit.

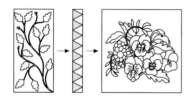

3. Sew a 2½" x 8½" dogtooth spacer to a vine block, then sew an 8½" x 8½" square to this unit.

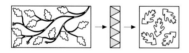

4. Sew an 8½" x 16½" vine block to a 16½" x 16½" feature block, then sew a 2½" x 24½" dogtooth spacer to this unit.

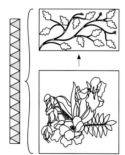

5. Sew the unit made in step 2 to the unit made in step 3.

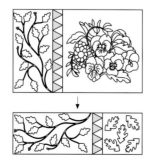

6. Sew the unit made in step 4 to the unit made in step 5.

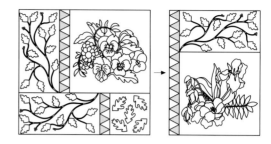

Section 2

1. Prepare, appliqué, and trim 2 feature blocks, 1 vine block, and 2 dogtooth spacers, each measuring 2½" x 16½".

2. Sew a dogtooth spacer between 2 feature blocks. Sew the second dogtooth spacer between this unit and a vine block to make Section 2 as shown.

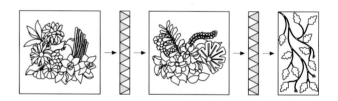

Section 3

1. Prepare, appliqué, and trim 2 feature blocks, 3 vine blocks, 1 block measuring 8½" x 8½", and 2 dogtooth spacers, each measuring 2½" x 24½".

2. Sew the 8½" x 8½" block to the end of a vine block.

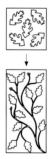

3. Sew a vine block to each remaining feature block.

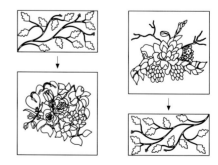

4. Sew a dogtooth spacer between each unit made in steps 1–3.

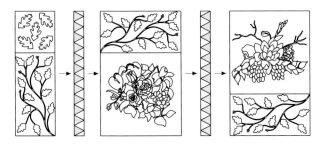

Assembling the Quilt Top

1. Sew Section 1 to Section 2, then Section 3 to Section 2.

Section 1

Section 2

Section 3

2. Following instructions for "Borders with Straight-Cut Corners" on page 34, measure, cut, and sew 2½"-wide side border strips to each side of the quilt. Repeat for top and bottom borders.

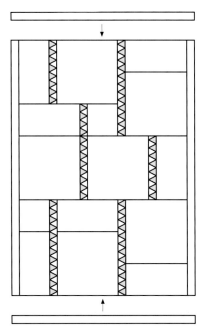

3. Following the instructions for "Borders with Mitered Corners" on page 35, measure and cut background and dogtooth fabric for the mitered dogtooth side borders.

❧ Note ❧

In addition to the extra length added for mitered borders, add 2" to the width and 4" to the length of each border strip to allow for shrinkage during appliqué. For example, for a 2"-wide (finished) border, cut the strips 4½" wide and add 4" to the mitered border length.

4. Measure and cut background and dogtooth fabric for the top and bottom mitered dogtooth borders.

5. Prepare and appliqué dogtooth borders.

6. After completing the appliqué, trim the border strips as necessary, then sew borders to the quilt.

7. Following instructions for the "Oak Leaf with Vines and Berries" border on page 69, measure, cut, appliqué, trim, and sew borders to the quilt.

8. Measure, cut, and sew 1½"-wide outer side borders to the quilt. Repeat for top and bottom borders.

9. Layer the quilt top, batting, and backing.

10. Baste the layers together. Quilt as desired.

11. Bind the edges.

A Gathering of Purple

Finished size: 40" x 40"
Block size: 8" x 8"
Color Photo: page 41

This small quilt is a perfect project for the appliqué beginner. When Marilyn Mowry, who appliquéd this quilt, started the class, she had never before appliquéd. It was a perfect combination—a beginner stitching the beginner's project!

Fabric Requirements

Background for 8" x 8" (finished) blocks	¾ yd.
Small setting triangles	⅞ yd.
Large side setting triangles and corners	1⅛ yds.
Sashing	⅜ yd.
Assorted fabrics for appliqué	¼ yd. each of 6 fabrics
For Vines (optional)	1 yd.
Batting	46" x 46"
Backing	1½ yds.
Binding	½ yd.

❧ Note ❧

Appliqué the large side setting triangles by adapting a vine motif from the complementary block "Vine with Leaves and Berries" on page 62. If you choose to appliqué these side setting triangles, add 2" to each dimension of the 21¼" x 21¼" square to allow for shrinkage during appliqué.

Cutting

The dimensions given for the following appliqué blocks are for cut size, before appliqué. The additional 2" to the cut size allows for shrinkage during appliqué.

   5 complementary blocks, each 10½" x 10½"
  10 sashing strips, each 1½" x 8½"
  10 sashing strips, each 1½" x 10½"
  10 squares, each 8" x 8", for setting triangles
   1 square, 21¼" x 21¼", for large side setting triangles
      (See note on page 75.)
   2 squares, each 10⅞" x 10⅞", for corner triangles
   5 strips, each 3" x 42", folded in half lengthwise for
      French binding (See page 82.)

Assembly

1. Prepare and appliqué 5 complementary blocks and trim to measure 8½" x 8½". Refer to the patterns for small complementary blocks, beginning on page 58.

2. Sew a 1½"x 8½" sashing strip to opposite sides of the block. Sew a 1½" x 10½" sashing strip to the remaining 2 sides.

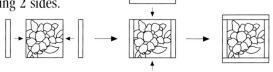

3. Cut each 8" x 8" square in half once diagonally to make 20 triangles.

Make 20.

4. Sew the long edge of each triangle to the block, being careful not to stretch bias edges.

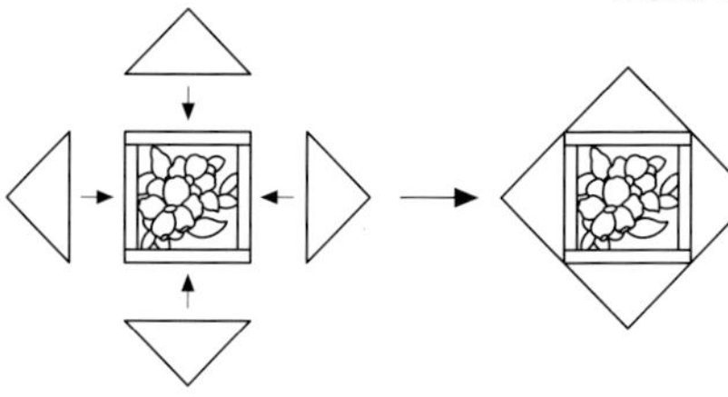

❧ Tip ❧

Fold the triangles in half and place a pin at the fold. Pin the center of the block. Match and pin centers first, then outer edges. Sew triangle to block.

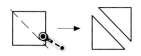

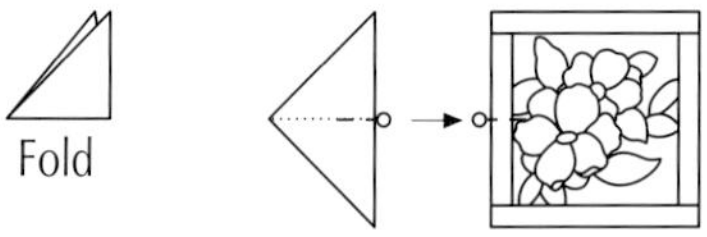

Fold

5. Cut the 21¼" x 21¼" square in half twice diagonally to make 4 side setting triangles.

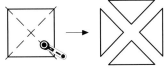

Make 4.

❧ Note ❧

If you wish to appliqué these triangles, draw seam allowance lines, appliqué the square first, trim to 21¼" x 21¼", then cut into triangles.

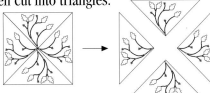

6. Sew the blocks together, adding side setting triangles as shown. Take care not to stretch bias edges. See Tip on sewing triangles to blocks on page 74.

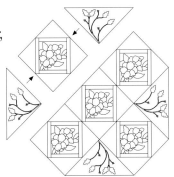

7. Cut each 10⅞" x 10⅞" square in half once diagonally to make 4 corner triangles. Sew the long edge of a triangle to each corner of the quilt. For appliquéd corners, appliqué the squares first, then cut them in half.

Make 4.

8. Layer the quilt top, batting, and backing.

9. Baste the layers together. Quilt as desired.

10. Bind the edges.

Images of Time

Finished size: 32" x 36"
Block size: 8" x 16"
Color photo: page 42

Peggy Cord selected seasonal colors for each vine block, coordinating the colors so that the wall hanging can be hung throughout the year.

Fabric Requirements

Background for 8" x 16" (finished)
    vine blocks .... ⅝ yd. each of 3 fabrics
Dogtooth sashing
    Background .... ⅜ yd.
    Dogtooth .... ⅛ yd. each of 7 gradations
Dogtooth borders
    Background .... ⅝ yd.
    Dogtooth .... ⅛ yd. each of 7 gradations
Assorted fabrics for appliqué
Vines (total) .... 1⅛ yds.
Leaves (4–6 fabrics) .... ¼ yd.
    each
Batting .... 38" x 44"
Backing .... 1⅛ yds.
Binding .... ⅜ yd.

Cutting

The dimensions given for the following blocks, sashing, and borders are for cut size, before appliqué. The additional 2" to the cut size allows for shrinkage during appliqué.

> 6 vine blocks, each 10½" x 18½"
> 2 dogtooth sashing strips, each 4½" x 32½"
> 2 dogtooth border strips, each 4½" x 40"
> 2 dogtooth border strips, each 4½" x 38"
> 4 strips, each 3" x 42", folded in half lengthwise for French binding (See page 82.)

Assembly

1. Following the instructions on page 62, prepare, appliqué, and trim the 8½" x 16½" vine blocks.
2. Sew the blocks together in 3 rows of 2 blocks each.

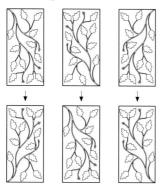

3. Prepare and appliqué 2 dogtooth sashing strips, following the instructions for "Dogtooth Spacers" on pages 65–67. Each triangle "tooth" measures 2" (finished) at the base. Trim each sashing strip to measure 2½" x 32½".
4. Sew a sashing strip between each set of vine blocks.

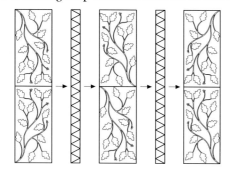

5. Following the instructions for "Borders with Mitered Corners" on page 35, measure and cut back-

ground and dogtooth fabric for the mitered dogtooth side borders.

❧Note❧

In addition to the extra length added for mitered borders, add 2" to the width and 4" to the length of each border strip to allow for shrinkage during appliqué. For example, for a 2"-wide (finished) border, cut the strips 4½" wide and add 4" to the mitered border length.

6. Measure and cut top and bottom dogtooth border strips.
7. Appliqué each dogtooth border.
8. After completing the appliqué, trim the border strips to measure 2½" wide and as long as necessary. (See "Borders" on pages 34–35 to figure length.) Sew borders to the quilt.
9. Layer the quilt top, batting, and backing.
10. Baste the layers together. Quilt as desired.
11. Bind the edges.

La Petite Fleur

Finished size: 51" x 33"
Block size: 8" x 8"
Color photo: page 43

Six floral complementary blocks provide a wonderful opportunity for the appliqué beginner to learn floral appliqué. The optional anemone border offers a challenge for the beginner and a treat for the appliqué enthusiast!

Fabric Requirements

Background for 8" x 8" (finished) blocks	¾ yd.
Setting triangles	⅞ yd.
Sashing and inner border	1 yd.
Corner squares	scraps
Anemones with Berries border background	¼ yd.
Outer border	¼ yd.
Assorted fabrics for appliqué	¼ yd. each of 12 fabrics
Batting	59" x 45"
Backing	1½ yds.
Binding	½ yd.

Cutting

The dimensions given for the following blocks and borders are for cut size, before appliqué. The additional 2" to the cut size allows for shrinkage during appliqué.

- 6 complementary blocks, each 10½" x 10½"
- 12 squares, each 8" x 8", for setting triangles
- 12 sashing strips, each 1½" x 8½"
- 12 sashing strips, each 1½" x 10½"
- 7 sashing strips, each 1½" x 14⅝"
- 2 cornerstones, each 1½" x 1½"
- 5 inner border strips, each 1½" x 42"
    (piece as necessary)
- 1 strip, 5½" x 36", for Anemones with Berries border
- 3 strips, each 2½" x 42", for outer borders
- 4 strips, each 3" x 42", folded in half lengthwise for French binding (See page 82.)

Assembly

1. Prepare and appliqué 6 complementary blocks, referring to the patterns on pages 58–61, then trim to measure 8½" x 8½".

2. Sew a 1½" x 8½" strip of sashing fabric to opposite sides of the block, then sew a 1½" x 10½" strip to the adjacent sides.

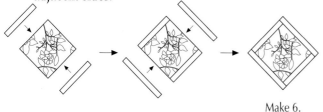

Make 6.

3. Cut each 8" x 8" square in half once diagonally to make 24 triangles.

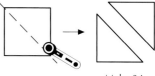

Make 24.

4. Sew 4 triangles to each block, sewing the long edge of each triangle to the block, being careful not to stretch bias edges. See Tip on page 74.

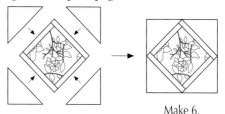

Make 6.

5. Sew a 1½" x 14⅝" sashing strip between two blocks for each row.

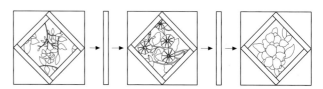

6. Sew a 1½" x 1½" cornerstone to each end of a 1½" x 14½" sashing strip, then sew a 1½" x 14½" sashing strip to each end.

7. Sew the sashing strip made in step 5 between each 3-block unit.

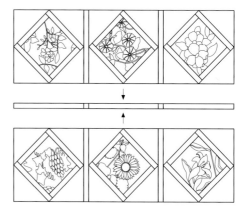

8. Piece together 1½"-wide inner border strips as required, then measure, cut, and sew a strip to the top and bottom of the quilt, referring to the directions given in "Borders with Straight-Cut Corners" on page 34.

9. Measure, cut, and sew a 1½"-wide inner border strip to each side of the quilt.

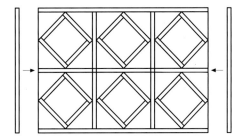

10. Measure, cut, and sew a 2½"-wide outer border strip to the top of the quilt.

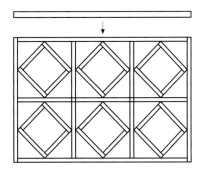

11. Cut a strip of background fabric, 5½" x 35". "La Petite Fleur," pictured on page 43 has an appliquéd border using part of the pattern given for the Anemones with Berries border on page 69. Select a portion of the pattern for appliqué and repeat the sequence as necessary to fit your border strip.

12. Trim the completed appliquéd border strip as needed, then sew to the left side of the quilt.

13. Measure, cut, and sew the 2½"-wide outer side border to the left side of the appliquéd border as shown.

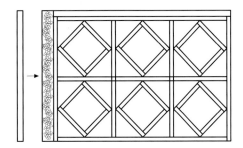

14. Layer the quilt top, batting, and backing.
15. Baste the layers together. Quilt as desired.
16. Bind the edges.

In Hope of Entwives

Finished size: 48" x 32"
Block size: 8" x 16"
Color photo: page 43

Susan B. Elliott set four vine blocks together to suggest an Art Deco feeling and gave it a name from Tolkien's *Lord of the Rings* series. Combined with zigzag dogtooth and appliquéd oak-leaf borders, the blocks make a lovely statement without being complex. Susan's quilt is entirely machine appliquéd, using the invisible machine appliqué method given in Roxi Eppler's book *Smoothstitch® Quilts: Easy Machine Appliqué* (That Patchwork Place). Susan also machine quilted this quilt.

Fabric Requirements

Background for 8" x 16" (finished)
  vine blocks .... ⅝ yd.
Zigzag dogtooth border
  Background .... ⅝ yd.
  Zigzag color A* .... ¼ yd.
  Zigzag color B* .... ¼ yd.
Assorted fabrics for appliqué
  Vines .... ⅝ yd.
  Leaves .... ¼ yd. each of 3 or 4 fabrics
  Flowers .... ⅛ yd. each of 4 fabrics
Inner and third border .... ⅜ yd.
Outer border .... 1⅛ yds.
Batting .... 36½" x 54"
Backing .... 1⅝ yds.
Binding .... ⅝ yd.
If using one color for zigzag, purchase ⅝ yard.

Cutting

The dimensions given for the following blocks, sashing, and borders are for cut size, before appliqué. The additional 2" to the cut size allows for shrinkage during appliqué.

    4 vine blocks, each 10½" x 18½"*

    3 strips, each 1" x 42", for inner side borders

    2 zigzag dogtooth border strips, each 2½" x 48"

    2 zigzag dogtooth border strips, each 2½" x 24"

    4 strips, each 1" x 42", for third borders

    6 strips, each 5½" x 42", for outer borders

    6 strips, each 3" x 42", folded in half lengthwise for
       French binding (See page 82.)

    Susan reduced the finished block size to 7½" x 15½"
    for an evenly spaced zigzag dogtooth border.

Assembly

1. Prepare and appliqué 4 vine blocks. Remember to reverse the pattern for 2 blocks. Trim to measure 8½" x 16". Sew blocks together to make 2 rows of 2 blocks. Sew rows together.

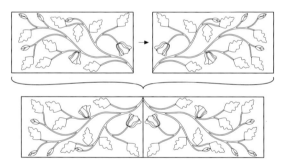

2. Following the instructions on page 34 for "Borders with Straight-Cut Corners," measure, cut, and sew 1"-wide side borders to the quilt. Measure, cut, and sew 1"-wide top and bottom border strips to the quilt top.

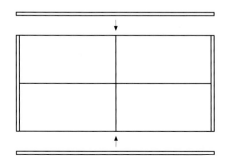

3. Following the instructions for mitered borders on page 35, measure and cut side zigzag and dogtooth border strips.

Note

Remember to add 4" to the measured length to allow for shrinkage during appliqué.

4. Measure and cut top and bottom dogtooth border strips.

5. Appliqué dogtooth border strips, following the directions for zigzag dogtooth spacers on pages 67–68. *The triangles in the quilt shown on page 43 measure 2¼" long on each side and are 2" high to fit the borders evenly.*

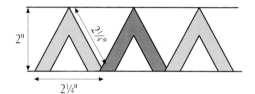

✣Tip✣

Use one background color for the zigzags, or use two or more colors. Susan alternated red and green fabrics for the zigzags, which she reverse-appliquéd, for a dynamic zigzag border.

6. After completing the appliqué, trim the border strips to measure 2½" wide and as long as necessary. Sew borders to the quilt top.

7. For the third border, measure, cut, and sew the 1"-wide top and bottom border strips to the quilt. Repeat for side borders.

8. For the outer border, measure and cut the 5½"-wide top and bottom outer border strips. Measure and cut the side border strips.

9. Appliqué this border as desired, leaving the corners free of appliqué until the borders have been sewn to the quilt.

⊸∾Note∾⊱

After the borders were added to the quilt, Susan designed and appliquéd a meandering vine. She included a ¼"-wide stem, 10 large oak leaves (use one of the leaves from the Oak Leaf block on page 58), and 4 flowers and a bud from the "Vine with Buds and Blossoms" block pattern on page 62.

10. Trim if necessary, then sew top and bottom borders to the quilt. Repeat for side borders.
11. Finish appliquéing the corners.
12. Layer the quilt with batting and backing.
13. Baste, then quilt as desired.
14. Bind the edges.

Barbara's Bloomin' Birthday

Finished size: 38" x 38"
Block size: 14" x 14"
Color photo: page 42

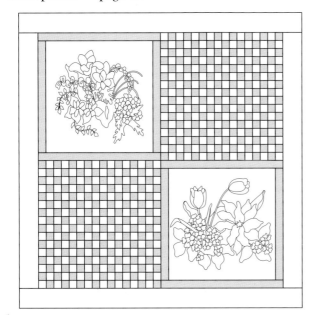

This setting for 2 blocks includes a pieced checkerboard background and makes a beautiful wall quilt to give to someone special. For a memorable gift, create your own optional finishing touches, such as an appliquéd or pieced border instead of the scalloped border shown.

⊸∾Note∾⊱

The feature blocks in this quilt measure 14" x 14" instead of 16" x 16" when finished. They were trimmed to 14½" x 14½" after appliqué. When choosing appliqué patterns for these blocks, make sure there will be enough background surrounding the appliqué to trim without cutting into the appliqué.

Fabric Requirements

Background	⅝ yd.
Color A for checkerboard (or use background fabric)	⅝ yd.
Color B for sashing and checkerboard	¾ yd.
Outer borders	½ yd.
Batting	42" x 42"
Backing	1¼ yds.
Binding	½ yd.

Cutting

The dimensions given for the feature blocks are for cut size, before appliqué. (Remember, the feature blocks in this quilt measure 14" x 14" when finished.) The additional 2" added to the cut size allows for shrinkage during appliqué.

2 feature blocks, each 16½" x 16½"
4 strips of color B, each 1½" x 14½", for sashing
4 strips of color B, each 1½" x 16½", for sashing
12 strips of color A, each 1½" x 42", for strip-pieced units
12 strips of color B, each 1½" x 42", for strip-pieced units
4 strips of color A, each 3½" x 42", for outer borders
5 strips, each 3" x 42", folded in half lengthwise for French binding (See page 82.)

Assembly

1. Prepare and appliqué 2 feature blocks; trim to 14½" x 14½". (See note on page 80.)

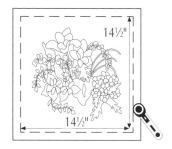

2. Sew a 1½" x 14½" sashing strip to each side of each block, then sew a 1½" x 16½" sashing strip to the top and bottom of each block.

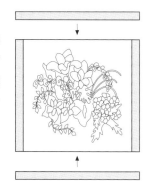

3. Alternating 4 strips each of color A and color B, sew 1½" x 42" strips into a strip-pieced unit as shown. Make 3 strip-pieced units.

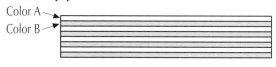

Make 3.

4. Cut across the strip-pieced unit at 1½" intervals to make 64 rectangles.

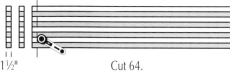

1½"   Cut 64.

5. Sew rectangles together in pairs, end to end, alternating colors as shown, to make 32 units, each measuring 1½" x 16½".

Make 32.

6. Sew together 16 of the units made in step 4, reversing alternate units to make a checkerboard square, measuring 16½" x 16½".

Make 2.

7. Sew blocks and checkerboard squares together.

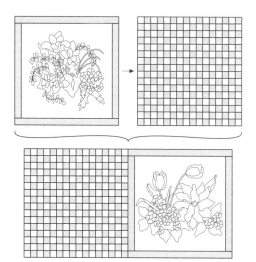

8. Following the directions given on page 34 for "Borders with Straight-Cut Corners," measure, cut, and sew 3"-wide border strips to each side of the quilt. Repeat for top and bottom strips.

❧Note❧

Instructions are given for a straight-edged outer border. The border shown in the photo on page 42 includes a gentle, random scallop with rounded corners, cut after the borders have been added to the quilt. To achieve a round corner, set a saucer, plate, or jar lid at each corner, trace around the edge, and cut. If you choose to scallop the borders on your quilt, use bias binding.

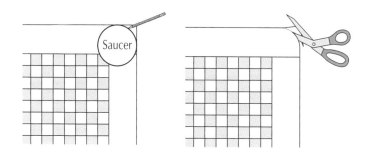

9. Layer the quilt top, batting, and backing.

10. Baste the layers together. Quilt as desired.

11. Bind the edges.

FINISHING TECHNIQUES

By the time we get the quilt top finished, we are often so enraptured with its beauty or so tired of the project that we shortchange the finishing process. I won't go into the technical aspects of these final steps; That Patchwork Place has published a very useful series of books that include *Loving Stitches* by Jeana Kimball, about fine hand quilting, and *Happy Endings* by Mimi Dietrich, covering binding and finishing techniques. Please refer to these two informative books for any questions that you may have on technique.

I'll confess here and now: Mimi, I still pull out *Happy Endings* when doing those inside points on scalloped-edge binding! Thanks for all the help—glad you were there.

A Few Words About Quilting

The quilting line holds together the textile sandwich of top, batting, and backing. It is far more than just a way to keep all the fabric held securely together. The quilting line usually contributes the final design element. In appliqué quilts, the quilting design should complement the appliqué without detracting from it.

Quilting around the individual flowers and leaves causes the batting to plump up inside those motifs, adding to the dimensional quality of the work. Quilting inside a design element flattens it. For the iris leaves on "In Bloom" on page 36, close quilting enhances the turning of the leaves.

Background quilting should draw attention to the blocks themselves in one of two ways, either by making the background recede or by pushing the flowers forward. Heavy quilting, such as cross-hatching, creates an overall texture for the viewer, causing the background to recede. Radiating lines, such as those found within the blocks of "In Bloom," draw the viewer's eye into the block, giving the flowers more attention.

Don't hesitate to change the scale of the design elements for any project. Linda Gillespie's quilt "Kaizen" on page 37 features highly contrasting, narrow diagonal lines that change direction within the body of the quilt. The geometry and scale of the lines contrast with the organic patterning of the blocks. In each of the blocks within your quilt, try something as simple as the same quilting pattern, cross-hatching for example, but vary the widths between the lines.

This combination of scale and patterning works well with an asymmetrical design in the quilting pattern. The change of texture offers additional stimuli, bringing viewers closer to the quilt and keeping them there, observing for a longer period of time.

If you have a camera handy, snap a few pictures of your finished quilt top. Make a few enlarged photocopies of the print and use these to play with while designing the quilting lines. This gives a better idea of the finished look without making all the mistakes.

Another good exercise to use for designing quilting lines is to think of the quilt top as a blank piece of paper. Forget about what is on the surface of the quilt top and place any design, no matter how unrelated, over the surface. In a pieced quilt, you can disregard the pattern completely and apply the quilting lines from side to side, top to bottom. If you choose to do this with an appliqué quilt, simply quilt the line up to the appliqué pattern, stop at the appliqué, tie off, and continue the quilting line on the other side of the appliqué.

A Few Words About Binding

Binding can also be used as a decorative element. Try using a striped fabric cut on the bias or a contrasting fabric for a colorful finish to any quilt. A contrasting binding running along the edge of a scalloped border adds a distinctive touch. French binding, which has a double layer of fabric, makes a sturdy binding that wears well.

❧Note❧

For French binding, fold the fabric strip, wrong sides together, in half lengthwise. Align the raw edges with the edges of the quilt and stitch with a ½"-wide seam allowance. Fold the binding over to the back of the quilt and sew the fold of the binding to the back.

Never underestimate the importance of the quilting line or binding. Give these last design elements thought and consideration. Push yourself to try unusual finishing techniques. Don't stop with the appliqué when the last word has yet to be spoken!

Having the Last Word

There is so much to say about the process of quiltmaking and what it has given me—great friends, yards and yards of fabric, and some of the biggest headaches (all of which, I might add, I created myself out of a sense of play). No matter what you enjoy the most, the process or the final product, I hope the concept of contemporary floral appliqué is one that you will explore beyond the pages of this book.

Never be concerned about mistakes. It is from mistakes that we learn the most. Without them, there is no change or growth.

I can hardly wait to see your next quilt.

Meet the Author

Gabrielle Swain is a studio quilt artist whose work has been shown nationally and internationally. She became a quiltmaker after a career in the performing arts and has never looked back.

The body of her work has been nontraditional, but appliqué has always been her technique of choice. *Appliqué in Bloom* combines her award-winning design skills with her love of appliqué.

Gabrielle and her husband, Ron, share their home in Texas with three sons and Dahli, the family cat. Gabrielle is one of the founding members of North Texas Quilt Artists and is also a member of the Studio Art Quilt Associates. She has taught locally and regionally for the past eight years.